Happiness and Leadership

Career Paths Vol. 4: Being a Leader and Being
Happy Go Hand in Hand

James Bellerjeau

A Fine Idea

Contents

Introduction

G reetings readers and congratulations! Simply by virtue of being here, you are already on the path to increasing your odds of success.

Success as a leader does not require you to be perfect. Your task is to be self-aware and deliberate in how you approach situations.

Armed with the tips presented here, perhaps you will pick one idea and apply continuous improvement principles to tip the odds of success in your favor. Slowly but surely, you can turn the tide to your advantage.

Your career can certainly make you happy, but too often people make themselves miserable in pursuit of their ambitions.

The happiest people I know are the ones who learn that success is not measured in money:

- Can you say you like, trust, and respect the people you work with?

- Is your work interesting, challenging, and valuable?

- And do you share values with a solid company that has a strategy for continued success?

Then you have all you need to be happy and successful in your career.

These articles are about ways to advance your career while paying attention to what will make you happy. You will find additional approaches to succeeding at work in the companion volumes **Thriving at Work** and **The Pragmatist's Rules for Work**.

Success at work is not necessarily the same as how to live a good life or achieve satisfaction. If you want to explore these topics more deeply, I recommend you spend some time with the **Pragmatic Wisdom** series.

Be well.

Chapter One

No One Said Life Is Fair

Things are this way, and we can deal with them without adding to our burdens by worrying about unfairness

W hen I was growing up, my dad had a standard response to my brothers and me whenever one of us complained about the never-ending ways that life was unfair:

No one ever said life was fair.

My dad's answer used to annoy me no end because it didn't seem like any kind of answer. "That's not fair!" we complained, and my dad said, "That's right."

With time, I better appreciate the wisdom in this approach.

I am reminded of what Mark Twain once said about his father: "When I was a boy of 14, my father was so ignorant I could hardly stand to have the old man around. But when I got to be 21, I was astonished at how much the old man had learned in seven years."

Is it fair when the fisherman pulls a fish from the sea, or the crow plucks a worm from the field? Is it fair when it rains on your wedding day? When your car gets a flat tire, your train is late, and your flight is canceled? When your incompetent but conniving colleague is promoted before you?

We could expand this list a long time, but I'll let you fill in the blanks in your mind.

It's never personal

No, it's not fair. But nor do we have to take it personally.

Things are this way, and we can deal with them without adding to our burdens by worrying about unfairness. We can make things better without first making them worse by complaining about them.

Now later in my own life, I realize my dad was a philosopher at heart. He was trying to pass on to me and my brothers an old message. Here's how I've since heard it from that model Stoic, Marcus Aurelius:

> *A cucumber is bitter — throw it away. There are briars in the road — turn aside from them. This is enough. Do not add, 'and why were such things made in the world?'*

Marcus Aurelius knew to remind himself of this fact whenever needed. Though he was Emperor of Rome, he needed it every day.

So take this as your own helpful reminder, from Aurelius, my dad, and me to you: "No one ever said life was fair."

If you can keep this thought foremost in your mind when bad things happen, chances are you'll not only be more successful in your career. You'll probably be happier, too.

Be well.

Chapter Two

How Not To Get Rich

The keys to wealth, health, happiness, and so much more, are small steps that you take gradually over long periods of time

M ost people think that the way to get rich is to earn more money.

"Well, duh!" I hear you say. "We didn't really need you to tell us that earning more money will help you have more money."

Perhaps. But let me give you another perspective.

I started my career as a corporate lawyer in one of those New York firms that get headlines every year for the outrageous salaries they pay starting associates.

What junior lawyer is worth US$200,000 per year when they know how to do exactly nothing? By the way, those are the current salaries, not what I made when I started!

To the junior lawyers themselves, if they have a shred of self-awareness and humility, they know this is a great scam and there must be some catch. There is a catch, and more than one.

To start, those junior lawyers will work hard, really hard. For me, this is when I first became acquainted with what a 100-hour week feels like. For the mathematically inclined among you, it is more than 14 hours a day, every day, with no weekends or days off.

In hindsight, I can be grateful for those initial grueling days. Why? Because no one else's idea of a long week could compare. When I started working only 60–80 hours a week as in-house counsel, it felt like a breeze. I genuinely considered a 40-hour week to be working part-time.

The other catch is that as outrageous as your starting salary was, the law firm was charging your time out to clients at a much higher rate.

- An annual billing of 2,000 hours, which when I started would have been considered modest,

- at an hourly rate of US$500, also not at all unusual these days for junior lawyers,

- means that your law firm is charging clients US$1 million for your services.

Yes, your firm must cover a lot of overhead, and they don't bill all your time, but that still leaves a tidy profit. The pyramid is highly leveraged on the backs of associates.

You can assume law firm partners are clever businesspeople in touting those headline salaries, which is why there are more than 80 US law firms with profits per partner of more than US$1 million.

Back to getting rich. You would think that earning a salary of US$200,000 per year, let alone US$1 million per year, would be a guaranteed path to riches. Alas, for many their salary is no indication of their likelihood to become wealthy.

Why should this be so, you ask?

Let's say you are a lawyer in New York City, as I was, a common location for such high-earners.

- Similar to most big cities, your taxes are high (easily 50 percent all-in)

- as is your cost of living (say 30 percent for housing, and another 10–15 percent for living expenses).

- You might be left with something like 5–10 percent of your gross income to spend.

Where does it all go? Many possibilities, among them these:

- You have a nanny, perhaps a cleaner;

- You take expensive trips because after all, you work so hard, you deserve to treat yourself on the rare times you take off;

- You have a second home because even though you are working crazy hours, you can't expect your family to sit around waiting for you in a small city apartment; and

- Those kids will need to go to college.

The far more relevant questions to ask in determining a person's propensity to become wealthy are these:

How much of your income are you able to save?

Can you manage to regularly spend less than you earn?

If you can spend less than you earn, and you start to invest your savings in low-cost funds that track the broader stock market, you will be on the path to leveraging the power of time and compound interest.

We have among us people who are well on the path to achieving independence at levels of wealth far below what we usually assume is necessary.

I refer to adherents of the "Financial Independence Retire Early" movement or FIRE. These people are proof that you do not need wealth as it is traditionally defined (in money) to be happy.

One way not to get wealthy is to think that you need a lot of money to be rich. Another way is to mistake your income for wealth and spend more than you earn.

The keys to wealth, health, happiness, and so much more, are small steps that you take gradually over long periods of time.

Spend less than you earn, no matter how much you earn, and you will be on a path to good things. Then it is just a matter of being patient.

Be well.

Chapter Three

For a Great Career, Pursue Happiness Rather than Ambition

Pursuing ambitions can be counterproductive to our job performance. Prioritizing happiness instead brings multiple benefits

It took me more than a decade working as a C-suite executive to appreciate that ambition was not the only way to drive my career.

Let me first describe my journey and then I'll tell you what I learned from it. You might find something in my experience that helps you manage your own ambitions.

I hope you also find that pursuing personal satisfaction can be a powerful driver of your career.

Steps in my career that drove personal learnings

I became the General Counsel of a billion-dollar public company at age 30, which is a big deal.

I nonetheless thought I needed to progress. For example, to become General Counsel of a bigger company, say an S&P 500 company. I thought that's what a career means: Always planning the next move.

There I was, ten years in. Prodded by ambition, I interviewed for and got offered that next General Counsel position.

It was only when I was wrestling with the decision to stay or go that I carefully reflected on what was important to me.

What really brought me satisfaction in my job and my daily life? I realized I valued three things most highly:

1. The **people** I work with — do I like, trust, and respect them?

2. The **work** I was doing — is it interesting, challenging, and valuable?

3. The **company** I was doing it for — do I have the same values, is the company successful, and do I believe in the company's strategy for future success?

I concluded that I would be a great fool to give up what I had right in front of me for mere ambition. I saw that I already possessed all the ingredients for happiness and satisfaction in life.

I thus declined the shiny new job and spent the next ten years being grateful for what I had and doing the best job I could where I was.

Along the way, we grew our share price more than 30-fold, outperforming the great majority of public companies, and several years ago my company joined the S&P 500.

When I stopped being driven by my ambitions I got further than where I originally thought I could.

Then when I turned 50, I decided to give up my General Counsel role entirely.

This was not career suicide. It was anything but. It was a careful, conscious choice I arrived at by following the thought process I describe below.

Initially, I worked part-time while running my company's sustainability program. The switch from law to sustainability was invigorating. Not only that, I got half of my life back to spend on "sunny hours and summer days":

Many a forenoon have I stolen away, preferring to spend thus the most valued part of the day; for I was rich, if not in money, in sunny hours and summer days, and spent them lavishly; nor do I regret that I did not waste more of them in the workshop or the teacher's desk. — Henry David Thoreau

Here are the key things I learned on my journey, and why I came to see ambition as the least helpful tool for driving career success.

Focus first on finding satisfaction

I learned to focus first on finding happiness and satisfaction in life. This need not (and I believe should not) be tied to rigid career goals.

We are ambitious because we think this will bring us happiness, but we make ourselves unhappy in the pursuit of our ambitions. If we first create the foundation for satisfaction in life, we can approach our ambitions in a different way.

I had this thought after discovering that attorneys have one of the of any job, at least in the United States.

And here's something even more interesting: increasing responsibility and higher income for lawyers has almost no correlation with their happiness and well-being.

That suggests there is something more to satisfaction than traditional career progression.

Career ambition can sabotage your satisfaction

There is a potential conflict between making progress in your career, which requires you to think ahead and try to change your situation, and being happy and satisfied right now in your daily life.

If you are too focused on the future, you can become unhappy with your current situation and so fail to bring your full effort and talents to your current job.

This is doubly unfortunate, because not only do you make yourself unhappy, but you are less likely to advance if you don't bring your best to your current job.

Happiness enhances your effectiveness

In contrast, persons who truly value what they have, and give their best at what they are doing, are both happy and are performing well.

Happy, positive people engage well with their colleagues, which makes them more likely to be considered for promotion. Similarly, people who bring their best to their current jobs every day are more likely to be given greater responsibility, which also leads to promotion.

Thus, by not blindly pursuing ambition, you create the conditions for becoming happy. Your happiness, in turn, creates the conditions for you to bring your best to the job. And your daily performance is what drives your career.

Follow advice that's passed the test of time

It is our human nature that either enhances or inhibits our performance. Our ambitions torment us while finding satisfaction makes us happy.

After I grasped this, I realized I could call upon the best advice for mastering human nature that humankind has developed over millennia.

I took inspiration from the Roman Stoics, as well as Buddhist and Zen philosophers. They each have some excellent advice for us to manage this dynamic.

Here's how I summarize my top three takeaways, along with source quotes that provided me with inspiration.

1. Be happy with what you have and don't be sad about what you don't have

Consider these inspirations for how to accept your current situation:

> *It is an invincible greatness of mind not to be elevated or dejected with good or ill fortune. A wise man is content with his lot, whatever it be — without wishing for what he has not.* — Seneca

Be content with what you have, rejoice in the way things are. When you realize there is nothing lacking, the whole world belongs to you.
— Lao Tzu

2. Do a good job in your current job

Next, on paying attention to what is in front of you:

If you work at what is before you, following right reason seriously, vigorously, calmly, without allowing anything else to distract you, expecting nothing, fearing nothing, but satisfied with your present activity according to nature, you will live happy. — Marcus Aurelius

Do not dwell in the past, do not dream of the future, concentrate the mind on the present moment. — Buddha

3. Decide for yourself what success means to you

If you follow this line of thought further, you realize that ambition for its own sake may be harmful.

Who said it is necessary or good to chase after bigger jobs, more responsibility, and more pay? Who are you doing it for?

And what will your ambitions cost you in terms of hours of the day, time spent with family and friends, and being true to your deeply held values?

No one is compelled to pursue prosperity at top speed; it means something to call a halt instead of pressing eagerly after favoring fortune. — Seneca

Wealth consists not in having great possessions, but in having few wants. — Epictetus

Modern-day philosophers have carried the torch onward. This bit of wisdom from Steve Jobs helped me take decisions consistent with my values even when those decisions seemed crazy to others, like giving up my General Counsel role at the peak of my power.

Your time is limited, don't waste it living someone else's life. Don't be trapped by dogma, which is living the result of other people's thinking. Don't let the noise of others' opinions drown out your own inner voice. — Steve Jobs

If you still want career advice...

All this said I do not want to talk anyone out of having ambition or looking for career progression. Rather, I want to help you avoid being blindly driven before the whip of ambition without really thinking about what will satisfy you.

In pursuing happiness you may still meet your ambitions but you are much more likely to become happy. What is it you really want?

Be well.

Chapter Four

Try Using Economics to Steer Your Life

The basic rules of competition apply in many areas of life beyond buying goods and services. Knowing this, make decisions accordingly

Y ou might greatly improve your quality of life by applying basic economic principles to key choices you make: Where to spend your time, what goals to pursue, and how to measure your success.

By understanding how supply and demand (or more simply, competition) applies to much of your life, you can compete more effectively. You do this by focusing on areas where you have a competitive advantage, which comes from more than your efforts and abilities. It also comes from where you apply your efforts and abilities.

Supply and demand help explain the world

To begin, let's consider a few basic economic principles. We see lots of evidence in the news and public debate that many people don't appreciate these simple rules:

- When demand for goods and services remains constant but supplies are scarce, the prices for those goods and services increase.

- When supplies for goods and services remain steady but demand increases, the prices for those goods and services increase.

- And when demand is high and supplies are short, prices can increase dramatically.

All this is another way of saying that competition for limited resources is real and has an impact on what things cost. When we look at changes in supply and demand, we're effectively measuring how stiff the competition is for the underlying goods and services.

The more people who are trying to buy a car, book a flight, or fill their tanks with gas, the more that competition for limited resources will result in prices going up.

High Demand, Low Supply

Prices
(Relative Competition)

Low Demand, High Supply

It's a simple concept, for all that its effects are widespread

The basic rules of competition apply in many areas of life beyond buying goods and services. When there is massive demand but only limited supply, competition will be fierce.

- This explains why it is hard to get into the top schools, join certain professions, or get jobs in fast-growing companies.

- It explains why some salaries are much higher than others, why it's so hard to get elected to political office, and why very few individuals become models, movie stars, or best-selling authors.

Competing when the odds are stacked against you, or not

Many of us spend most of our time focused on the same things: money, power, fame, possessions. We have been dazzled by the supposed prizes and are blinded to the opportunity costs and likelihood of achieving them.

Economics offers another way of running the equation to achieve success: Look to places where competition is much scarcer (i.e., demand is lower), but where the rewards are still great.

At its heart, Stoicism offers such a refuge: Little competition for great rewards. These rewards are not the same as others chase. You will not hear a Stoic telling you to pursue a big bank account and a corner office, although these things may come.

Instead, set your sights on attaining wisdom and you will be amazed at how wide open the field is. You do not need to compete for scarce resources, because few others are looking for the same goal.

Not only that, but competition on the path to wisdom does not make your task harder. The more people seeking wisdom, the more you can support and benefit each other. Wisdom is one of the few areas in life where greater demand creates greater supply.

The reward for seeking wisdom

Best of all, the reward for seeking wisdom is a well-ordered mind following reason. Specifically, with wisdom, you will be satisfied and happy without regard to any of the scarce prizes your colleagues run after. Realizing you do not need money, job titles, or possessions to be happy is incredibly liberating.

The question to ask is: Do you want to be successful as it is traditionally understood, or do you want to be happy? The difference lies in whether you seek to attain wisdom.

You see what I did there. You thought you were getting an economics lesson, but instead, we used economics as a foothold into a Stoic principle. But my goal with both approaches was the same: to explore ways to live a good life and achieve satisfaction.

I can't guarantee you'll become wise if you diligently pursue wisdom as a goal. But the odds are in your favor.

Be well.

Chapter Five

How Will You Be Remembered?

If you want to know how you'll be remembered, it helps to understand how people think

First, I will point out an irony. That is, if you are overly worried about your legacy, chances are you will be challenged to leave a positive one.

The best people do not always seem to generate the broadest influence, but their impact on those they do influence is deep.

If you want to know how you'll be remembered, it helps to understand how people think.

A certain percentage of the population will tell you that people are defined by their exceptional moments.

- It is your best accomplishments in a long line of mundane events that people will remember.

Similarly, no matter how impressive your overall record is, these are the same people who will tell you that a person is also defined by their worst moments.

- An off-color joke, an offensive tweet, or a politically incorrect view. Any of these can be taken as evidence of your flawed nature, outweighing an otherwise unblemished life and character.

It is true that many people notice just the headlines, good or bad. Nowadays we can think of these fleeting headlines scrolling across our screens as social media moments.

But only shallow people think what they read in the headlines defines a person or even gives you a semi-realistic idea of what they stand for.

Would you want your life judged by strangers who know nothing about you?

Or worse, that they judge you by what other people are saying about you? I can't imagine many people would rush to sign up to such a standard. And yet it is a standard that people apply routinely without a second's thought.

It really takes only a brief reflection to arrive at a more well-founded conclusion.

Deeper thinkers know people are far more than the sum of their worst (or best) moments.

People are complex, yet we're capable of change.

If that weren't so, there would be no need for school, no need for training, and no need for a great deal of what humans do.

Strangers don't know a fraction of what makes you special and important. Thus, what strangers think of you based on misleading headlines designed to garner attention is far less meaningful than what people closest to you think of you.

When it comes to the people who do know you, the question becomes what impact did you make on them?

Were you kind and patient?

Did you listen to them when they were hurting and needed help? Did you help develop them and promote them in their careers?

Did you celebrate their successes, and commiserate with their failures? In short, did you act in ways to make their lives better?

If you had a positive impact on people close to you, rest assured your legacy is secured.

Perhaps not among the masses, who are easily distracted by superficial things. But people you genuinely care about and help are the ones who count.

I remember coming across a quote years ago from the Athenian statesman Solon, who was commenting on how to evaluate the lives of successful individuals. Solon's observation was this:

Count no man happy, until he is dead [or until the end is known].

Solon's point was that life is full of reversals of fortune. A person who is riding high now may later have a fall from grace. They may lose their wealth, they may fall ill, they may be caught up in a power struggle with the losing side, and so on.

According to Aristotle, to truly evaluate the success of a person's life and decide whether they achieved their highest good or eudaimonia, you should even extend your evaluation to look at their children's and relatives' lives.

For today, I think we can draw this lesson: You don't know what a person's life means until they have lived it out. You can tell very little from an isolated incident or a snapshot in time.

If you would not be judged by your worst moment, do not be quick to judge others for theirs.

Be well.

Chapter Six

Regret ... and Other Things That Compound

The power of compounding applies to our thoughts as much as it does to our actions

Many of you will know about the power of compound interest. Albert Einstein supposedly called it the "eighth wonder of the world" and Warren Buffet said, "My life has been a product of compound interest."

I've already referred to compounding for you in articles describing how to get rich. If you were reading carefully, then you understood that, although you can use compounding to achieve financial wealth, that will not necessarily bring you happiness.

If you want to be successful in your career, one of the most important things you can learn is that you are largely a creation of habits.

- Whether you succeed in your endeavors, feel happy with your life, and become physically and mentally healthy — all these things are driven by habits.

- Or as Raj on the sitcom The Big Bang Theory puts it when asking a girlfriend for honest feedback: "... except for anything I say, or do, or am. Those are my triggers."

Replace triggers with habits, and you grasp the importance of habits.

Without consciously realizing it, the little things we do become things that we regularly do. Things we regularly do compound over time. It is not just financial decisions that compound.

If you look, you will find compounding in these areas of your life as well:

- Small decisions you make each day about how you approach your work will impact the course of your career. Do you make a conscious choice to do your level best each day, no matter what you're doing? Or do you resent doing less exciting or less important work because you know you can do more?

- Your routine daily interactions with those around you will determine the course of your relationships. Do you treat your friends and family as gifts, and cherish them? Or do you take them for granted, and sometimes vent your frustrations on them?

- Anyone who has struggled to maintain their weight knows that it is small, daily decisions about what you eat that drive your long-term health.

- Similarly, if you've ever gotten on an exercise kick, you will have felt first-hand the wonderful reinforcement that comes from sticking with an exercise program and seeing the impact on your fitness.

The power of compounding applies to our thoughts as much as it does to our actions. If you dwell on your mistakes and wallow in regret, you will become a bitter person.

We all know someone who cannot let go of a past relationship or a missed opportunity. Does this make them fun to be around, even to themselves?

Do you want to be a sad, angry person? When you are stuck in the past, that means you are not living in the present.

Change is possible

My suggestion to you is that your nature is not immutable. Far from it. No matter what ill winds blow your way, you are more than the sum of what's happened to you.

If you wish, you can become a more positive, charitable, kind, and happy person. You don't even need the iron willpower of a Stoic master to do it.

All you need is to recognize that the power of habits applies to your mind and your thoughts. You can then start to adopt habits that move you in the direction you want to go.

The only thing you truly control is what you think. Thus, the path to happiness is not built upon pavers of enjoyment, but from choices: You must decide what you want and stick with your decisions.

You might be thinking, "This all sounds great in theory. But how do I control what I think in practice? Negative thoughts come to me unbidden."

To start, try to recognize when you find yourself dwelling on negative thoughts, or being uncharitable to others.

Also notice when you are being uncharitable to yourself. We are never so strict taskmasters as when we are judging our own actions.

Focus on the positive

Over time, you will become adept at catching yourself when you start to think negative thoughts. The next step is to consciously focus on something positive, no matter how trivial it seems. You can almost always find a positive in every situation.

Treat it as a challenge to find something good in even the seemingly worst possible situation. Relatively soon, you will have trained yourself to look for the positive. A setback suddenly becomes an opportunity, a hardship, a chance to test your mettle.

This practice is doubly helpful. It will move you in the direction of becoming a happier and more self-sufficient person. It also helps prepare you for the inevitable setbacks and hardships that come your way.

Be well.

Chapter Seven

Would You Rather Win the Silver or Bronze Medal?

Do you understand how much your desires are themselves contributing to your unhappiness?

B y now you know this is probably a trick question. But it illustrates a really important point that, if you can master, will help keep you on the path to happiness. First, some background.

Until recently I thought the so-called "replication crisis" was limited to the field of psychology.

The crisis refers to the fact that many published studies of scientific results cannot be reproduced by others who perform the same study at a later time. This depressed me because my undergrad was in psychology. Was it all a waste of time?

As it turns out, many fields besides psychology suffer from the problem that published scientific results are difficult to reproduce by others. Studies in medicine, marketing, economics, and now hard sciences are each falling prey to the problem of unrepeatability.

But there is one lovely little area of psychological research that has seen its results replicated, several times. It concerns the reactions of Olympic medalists to finding out if they've won gold, silver, or bronze.

- As could be expected, gold medalists are quite delighted. "I'm the best in the world, baby. Beat that."

- Bronze medalists are also outrageously happy on average, and good for them.

- If you've any sympathy in you, save it for the poor silver medalists. In some disciplines, their reactions ranged from despair to contempt, to nothing.

"Nothing, really?! You just won a freaking silver medal in the Olympics."

The space between

What explains this amazing reaction?

The studies refer to the athletes running "counterfactuals" in their heads, i.e. they compare their achievement to *what could have been*.

I've told you before that while people don't evaluate things well in isolation, we are excellent when it comes to comparing two things. The difference in the silver and bronze medalists' reactions can be explained by their comparison groups.

The silver medalist is looking at the tiny distance that separates them from the gold medalist.

- If only they could have eked out a few milliseconds more, they could be the champion.

- In this comparison, they forget that they've just beaten out every other person on the planet but one.

The bronze medalist, by contrast, is looking at the tiny distance that separates them from fourth place and everyone behind them.

- "My goodness," they think. "Only milliseconds separated me from not getting a medal at all."

- They look at all the others they have vanquished to become an Olympic medalist.

In other words, what you feel about a situation depends on where you direct your gaze.

Are you looking upward at what you could have achieved but did not? Or do you consider how far you have come and how many others you have outperformed?

Now for all of you who are not Olympic medalists or hopefuls, guess what? The same phenomenon applies to all of us in our daily lives.

Are you happy with your house, your job, your spouse, your salary, your neighborhood, your schools, your children, your pet, and on and on? It's not an objective standard, but rather a relative one.

If you're reading this, you're living in a time when more people have more freedom, security, and material goods than at any time in human history.

- Some 10 billion people who lived before you had a comprehensively tougher time, not to mention living lives that were "solitary, poor, nasty, brutish, and short."

- And you're complaining because your internet speed is too slow and there's nothing on Netflix?

Desires contribute to unhappiness

Do you understand how much your desires are themselves contributing to your unhappiness?

Have you realized how little the things you attain actually contribute to your long-term happiness? To make yourself unhappy by wanting things that will not make you happy is not a recipe for success.

By all means, aim for gold. But on the way, don't forget to appreciate what you have already achieved in your life and in your career. And remember how much better you have it than countless others.

Or to say it once more because it bears repeating: Be thankful for what you have, and don't be sad for what you don't have.

Be well.

Chapter Eight

It's Good To Be the Boss!

Of all the things that come with a promotion and a senior title, the one you should spend the most time contemplating is this: Responsibility

There are lots of reasons why it's just great being a senior manager. Here are a few common ideas people have about the benefits that come with the title:

> *Finally, I'll be able to just **make decisions** myself, without having to worry about what my boss or others think.*

> *Ah, I can't wait to have the **authority to implement** my priorities. People will have to do what I say!*

> *People will **listen to me** and respect my opinion because of my position. No more fighting for attention.*

My more experienced colleagues are no doubt laughing out loud right now. Or at least ruefully shaking their heads. And for good reason.

Of all the things that come with a promotion and a senior title, the one you should spend the most time contemplating is this: Responsibility.

- To make decisions is to have responsibility for the outcomes your team achieves.

- To exert authority to implement decisions is to bear responsibility for the resources your team expends.

- And to command authority by virtue of your position is to be responsible for what you say in every setting.

And that's assuming you actually are free to make decisions, exert authority, and have your opinion heard.

Let's explore the real world of your work environment for a moment.

Freedom

As a senior manager, you are *never* free of others' expectations when you make decisions.

You may be the senior-most legal officer, sure, but you still are bound by fiduciary responsibilities and must interact collegially with your other management peers.

Your tenure will be brief if you are oblivious to the toes you step on when making decisions. Not to mention the CEO and the board of directors are looking over your shoulder at every step.

(Lest you think there is yet a higher level at which you are ultimately free of such expectations, the CEO bears the cross of the board, and the board members ultimately answer to shareholders.)

Authority

So if you are not really free to make your decisions without considering the context, your fiduciary duties, and your various stakeholders, can we at least grant that you are much better positioned to *implement* your decisions?

To this, let me simply ask "Have you ever observed a parent interacting with a cranky toddler in a store?"

The parent clearly has all the structural authority in the relationship. They can direct the outcome by force. Yet witness how often the child prevails.

And before you blame this on poor parenting, turn now to your workplace. Can you think of a time that you yourself defied or ignored a company policy because it did not fit reality, was poorly designed, or was just plain "stupid"?

One of the things I liked most about working at a company with lots of engineers and scientists is that they are logical and methodological. If you can explain the reason and the rationale for your proposal, they will be faithful allies and excellent partners.

Now instead try to force such colleagues to implement your policy just because you say so and see what happens.

Your work colleagues have improved upon the tricks the cranky toddler employs to such great effect. If you try to force them to your will, you will meet with noncompliance that makes your hair prematurely gray and fall out.

I recently came across a line Desiderius Erasmus wrote in a letter to Sir Thomas More in 1521. The context was Martin Luther's agitation that led to the Protestant Reformation, and whether Church authorities should permit debate or force adherence to the current doctrine:

> *It is no great feat to burn a little man. It is a great achievement to persuade him.*

What was true 500 years ago is still true today: You must persuade, never dictate.

Being heard

And to our final point, will you have authority by virtue of your position? Will people listen to you as a result of your role?

Here I can give more positive news. Yes, they will, at least at first.

For them to keep listening, you must do both of the following:

- You must listen carefully and ask relevant questions to tease out the real issues, for the full set of issues is rarely contained in the initial request.

- Then you must provide pragmatic advice that demonstrates you understand the context and have placed the company's interests first.

In other words, you have to be good at your job if you expect people to listen to you. Your position just gets you the first "at bat." Everything after that is up to you.

It is unquestionably good to be the boss because it puts you in a position to influence your company.

But if you take your job seriously, you'll soon see that little comes with the title beyond the responsibility to live up to others' expectations.

I am confident you can do it. In fact, I expect nothing less.

Be well.

Chapter Nine

Why It's So Important to Develop Principles

I will save you the decade or so I spent following what turned out to be mostly fads. There is a simpler, better way to grow

B ad advice will be given to the new manager. By this, I mean a great mound of well-meant, but ultimately useless advice.

I will save you the decade or so I spent following what turned out to be mostly fads. There is a simpler, better way to grow.

But to fully appreciate the simple path, you must first understand the pitfalls that lie on the new manager's road.

Categories of bad advice

Here are some categories of advice I believe are as likely to lead you astray as help you:

- Almost everyone's first-hand explanation of what made them successful

- Almost all articles in management and business journals

- Most psychology or economics research unearthing some surprising quirk of human thinking or behavior

You can identify potentially bad advice from among the following characteristics:

- It is largely anecdote-driven

- It contains statistics expressed as percentages and only few absolute numbers

- It is included in a best-selling book with a dust-jacket blurb from Bono, Bill Gates, or Barack Obama. (Not to pick on these three fine individuals.)

Most of all, bad advice falls in the set of suggestions described as "This worked for Successful Person X or Company Y; try it and you can be successful too!"

Because we humans are fantastic pattern-recognition machines, we seek patterns everywhere and we find them everywhere. This would be wonderful except that we regularly assume causation in the face of nothing more than correlation.

We are easily taken in by anecdotes and stories because they trigger our pattern recognition function. We recognize a pattern, and we are primed to look out for the moral or lesson of the story.

What to do with others' success stories

You should consider one person's description of success to be an interesting story, nothing more.

That person experienced a unique situation, with unique challenges and opportunities, and brought to bear their special skills and experiences.

That person encountered far more randomness than they realized in each of their settings, their actions, and the outcomes of those actions.

Even if you could replicate their actions precisely (which you cannot because you are your own person), what are the chances that you will be in a similar enough situation and not be influenced by a different set of random interactions?

Why fads sell

Management and business journals are in the business of selling advertising, which means they need to drive viewers. Surprising and interesting stories attract eyeballs and clicks.

The truth of those stories is of secondary interest. Turns out that if you tell people what they want to hear and occasionally titillate them with something surprising along the way, they'll read your stories.

How about scientists? Can we take refuge among tenured professors, the scientific method, and peer-reviewed journals?

- Alas, you must be vigilant. Most published studies cannot be replicated, in most fields.

- Even studies with some validity are blown out of proportion in the push to publish.

- And reporters describe findings sensationally and without context because they want to grab your attention.

Focus on your own situation, skills, and experiences

In the business context, such advice from individuals, journalists, and experts is more than not useful.

It's downright harmful because it distracts you from focusing on what you could be more profitably doing.

"And what is that?" you ask. It is to focus on your own situation, your own skills and experiences, and your own challenges and opportunities.

What works for someone else is unlikely to work for anyone else because others are not you and others are not facing what you are facing.

But what works for you is something *you* should focus intensely on: How did you make that decision, why did it work (or often, not work), and what will you do differently next time?

Carefully observe your thought process and your decision-making process. Write down the principles that you are following. Discuss them with your colleagues on your team and refine them over time with the direction you'd like to take.

When I ran a legal team, I described our Legal Team Principles, called the Six Ps, as follows:

- **Proactive** — We address risks as early as possible.

- **Protective** — We protect the company's long-term interests.

- **Pragmatic** — We take informed risks.

- **Purposeful** — We work on high-risk and high-value topics.

- **Plain** — We seek to reduce complexity.

- **Powerful** — We follow continuous improvement principles.

To someone outside our team, this may look like a list of virtually useless buzzwords.

To me, it was a framework helping us decide among many competing priorities. It contained the seeds of our values and our mission. It reminded us to only work on topics that were directly supportive of the company's strategy.

I am not recommending the Six Ps to you as candidates for your own principles. I am suggesting that you spend time first considering and then committing your own principles to paper.

By focusing on how you make decisions and what you are doing in your unique situation, and then describing and improving your principles, you can drown out the distracting noise of others' unhelpful advice.

The only advice I'd like you to consider is this: You know how to improve your own results better than anyone else.

Be well.

Chapter Ten

Do You Have a "More" Mindset?

When we do not dwell in the past or daydream about the future, we open ourselves to the possibility of finding tranquility and joy

We live in times of abundance and surplus when standards of living are higher for more people than they have ever been.

How puzzling then that so many people are unhappy with their lot. I think you can lay the blame at the feet of our ambitions.

Although striving for material progress served humanity well for centuries by raising us out of widespread poverty into wealth, today it may be causing more harm than good. Let's explore why.

Why are we so ambitious?

We are ambitious because humans at heart are driven by relative status. We live in hierarchies, which are a fundamental facet of every society.

For a long time, accumulating material wealth was a way to show you were successful. And the more wealth, the more successful, apparently without any rational upper limit.

Thanks to both normal distributions of ability and the Pareto principle, a small percentage of people will be disproportionately successful in whatever dimension you measure, including earnings and wealth.

In the last few generations, and largely because most people no longer lack basic material goods, we've seen some interesting tweaks to the game of jockeying for status.

- Today a person can demonstrate high social status through a commitment to a cause, for example, climate change.

- Other topics that allow in-group members to lay claim to moral high ground include political party or religion, diversity, inclusion, and equity, or anti-racism and critical race theory.

What these all have in common is that they do not require anything other than passion and self-identification to have the desired signaling effect.

The ultimate aim for signing on to some of these causes may be to redistribute resources in different ways. Or to gain power and be able to be in charge of many of the decisions that will arise within working for the causes.

But in the short term, the social signaling aspect is a powerful reward in itself.

The problem with social virtue signaling as a status symbol is similar to that of accumulating wealth: "More" is better and there is no logical stopping point at which one can say enough is enough.

Hence, we see people taking ever more radical positions to demonstrate they care more than others. Our current polarized politics are one manifestation, as are the fights you see in schools over systemic racism training, and in companies over unconscious bias and diversity training.

The danger of comparing to others

My point is not to criticize any particular cause or social group — they almost all have basic validity at some level.

Rather, I want to draw attention to the idea that if you seek your relative value or worth in comparison with others, you are demonstrating a "more" mindset: If only I had more _____, I would be happy.

Is there another way? How about living fully in the moment?

When we do not dwell in the past or daydream about the future, we open ourselves to the possibility of finding tranquility and joy in what we are doing right now.

Success can mean saying "No"

I recently came across an example of a person who was successful at almost everything he tried, including things that appeared impossible before he came along and did them.

The genius mathematician, Edward O. Thorp, demonstrated that it was possible to beat the house playing blackjack, and then went on to spearhead the quantitative trading movement in financial markets, becoming wealthy in the process.

His book *A Man For All Markets* is fantastic reading.

More impressive than his many intellectual and financial accomplishments, at least to me, were his decisions to stop playing the game.

Thorp recognized that a "more" mindset could never be satisfied and so thought about what was important to him in life. In his own words:

> *To preserve the quality of my life and to spend more of it in the company of people I value and in the exploration of ideas I enjoy, I chose not to follow up on a number of business ventures, although I believed that they were nearly certain to become extremely profitable.*
> – Edward O. Thorp

The Stoic philosopher, Seneca, would celebrate Thorp, not for his many material accomplishments, but for having identified what was important to him and behaving accordingly.

If that meant leaving money and accolades on the table, so be it. In this way, Thorp serves as one of the many good examples that we can follow.

You're already there

The only thing I would wish you to seek more of is satisfaction. Your happiness will come from paying attention to what you are doing at the moment you are doing it.

We do not need to be geniuses to follow in the footsteps of geniuses. They have blazed a path for us, and all we need to do is follow. It is up to us to choose our paths accordingly.

Be well.

Chapter Eleven

What Should We Wish For?

Perhaps we should wish for something other than more of the promotions, wealth, and possessions that aren't making us happier

I used to sign farewell cards at work with something like: "I wish you every success in your new endeavors."

Now, when I think back, this was wrong to write.

- A person who is successful at everything has no reason to question the foundation of their happiness.

- They have material wealth, and career success, and seem to have it all.

- But such persons are at great risk of identifying their happiness with those external things.

Failure and setbacks are normal

What happens when life knocks a pillar out from underneath a person who's known nothing but success?

Say they suffer a career setback, a health issue, or have relationship troubles. It can be devastating. They become unhappy and cannot be happy again until the external situation is fixed.

If getting everything we want carries its own pitfalls, what should we wish for others to achieve?

Let's say you are a caring boss, and you want your colleagues to succeed at work. What does that success actually mean?

- Does it mean they never make a mistake?

- Or is it better that they learn from the small mistakes they make and so become wiser?

Promotions are not the true measurement of success

Does success mean an employee advances from one promotion to the next, scaling the heights of power? Or would you wish that they come to appreciate the deep satisfaction from doing their existing jobs ever better?

Does success mean they make more money than their peers in other companies? Or are they better off learning early that their worth is poorly measured in money?

Wish what parents wish for their children

What about what parents wish for their children?

If you ask the kids themselves, many will tell you they want to be rich, powerful, or famous. Sometimes all three.

It takes the age and experience of parents to wonder if a far more valuable gift would be that their children are happy, find love, or make a lasting contribution to society.

I suspect you've noticed people who never seem satisfied with what they've achieved. You may have managed employees who are always itching for more: responsibility, pay, and promotions.

I've noticed the desire for more does not seem to correlate with talent. That is, all sorts of people fall prey to being dissatisfied with their current position, the gifted and the striving alike.

External wants don't satisfy

It's usually easy for a boss or a parent to offer sound advice to a colleague or their child:

- Be careful placing your hopes and dreams in external things like wealth, power, or fame.

- When you set any of these as your goal, you set yourself on a path of guaranteed hardship and likely disappointment.

Goals are a declaration of what you want, not a blueprint for how to get there. Moreover, when you set a goal, you are opening yourself up to a potentially long period of unhappiness until you reach your goal.

You may find that the cost of achieving your goal far outweighs the benefits, but you realize this only after the damage has been done.

Taking the larger perspective, we live in times of great abundance. Most of us have demonstrably more wealth, health, and possessions than humans across the vast march of time. We have also advanced the state of our collective knowledge to unprecedented heights.

How do we explain then that we simultaneously find ourselves irritated and annoyed to distraction?

We chafe and argue with one another and believe we are surrounded by dangerous idiots. We feel that our own success remains out of reach, and we run harder chasing after it.

A tranquil mind

Perhaps we should wish for something other than more of the promotions, wealth, and possessions that aren't making us happier.

I think we'd do well to give ourselves the same advice we'd give our colleagues and our children: To experience lasting joy — and not just fleeting enjoyment — we must remember that joy does not come from external things but from a tranquil mind.

> *When you are free from doubt, worry, jealously; when your course is the same whether you are pushing into the headwind or blown along by a tailwind; when you delight in stillness as much as you do in motion; when you do not rely on external things, joy is your reward.*

So the next time you sign a farewell card, consider writing something like this:

"I wish you a string of small failures that teach you to be mindful so as to fully appreciate all that you already have, the people you're lucky enough to spend time with, and whatever you're doing at exactly this moment."

Or if that's too long, you can just say "Be well" and hope they fill in the blanks themselves.

Be well.

Chapter Twelve

Who Are the Most Cost-Effective Employees?

Because humans are complex and varied, the safeguards put in place to protect us themselves create opportunities for mischief

C an a company rationalize discrimination?

Healthy societies foster freedom of thought and freedom of expression. We can make the world a better place through our ideas, and this requires us to share them. It is in this spirit that I offer today's discussion.

I explain my thinking with a series of hypotheses. You may agree or not with any of them, but at least you'll understand my thought process.

I'll show how an organization could easily justify preferentially hiring and promoting a certain type of employee.

Hypothesis 1 — It is economically rational for companies to consider their total costs when hiring and promoting employees.

These costs can include brand and reputation impacts associated with the composition of a company's workforce.

There is a strong argument that having diverse employees leads to better business outcomes (although hard data demonstrating causation is thin on the ground).

Furthermore, companies that lack diversity risk alienating stakeholders.

Hypothesis 2 — Some employees cost their companies more than others even though they perform the same work.

Costs here include not just an employee's salary and benefits, but also the risks and friction associated with the company managing that employee.

It takes time and costs money to respond to employee concerns, complaints, and lawsuits. Here are several examples.

- Employees may oppose the company pursuing legal business with customers they object to, which could include any "out-of-favor" group or industry. We sometimes see this in younger employees or those who simply may have more of their idealism intact. For as many opinions as individuals have about the world, some employees expect the company's business to reflect their opinions. This is understandable, but the attendant controversy is costly. Either the company voluntarily reduces its business, or it risks losing employees and customers who disagree with its decision not to cut off other customers.

- Whenever an individual is promoted, you can expect some employees to think that other, more qualified, individuals were overlooked. Because individuals' perception of their own performance is biased, any merit-oriented organization will suffer from concerns about these decisions. This puts companies in no-win situations: They either let the issue blow over, which means living with a certain number of disgruntled employees, or they give reasons why the non-promoted persons were not as qualified, making them and their promoters doubly unhappy.

- Next, because individuals' understanding of their own versus others' relative work contributions is incomplete, any merit-oriented organization will suffer from concerns about unequal pay. Paying two individuals differently for what appears to be similar work is unequal pay, so complaints are easy to make. Many complaints are justified. But responding to such complaints is fraught with risk. Companies either demonstrate that individuals' market value and how their contributions differ, demotivating the less valuable employee, or they avoid the argument by simply adjusting pay to eliminate gaps, demotivating the employees making greater contributions.

- Lastly, we have strong laws protecting many groups against unlawful discrimination. In the United States, companies may not discriminate on the basis of race, color, sex, or age, among other things. Call these groups "protected classes." Protected classes can have different costs, as I explain below.

It is necessary and appropriate for individuals to raise legitimate concerns about discrimination. This helps keep companies honest. But because humans are complex and varied, the safeguards themselves create opportunities for mischief. Here's how.

Although most people are honest and ethical, some percentage is not. Behavioral economics predicts that when rewards for cheating exist, some number of people always cheat. They take advantage of loopholes to gain a personal advantage.

A dishonest employee can put considerable pressure on their employer by claiming discrimination even where none exists.

If even a few employees in protected classes exploit legal protection to obtain negotiation leverage, promotions, or settlements, companies' costs rise for all employees in that class.

Hypothesis 3 — Some people are dishonest, and a few bad apples cause harm to all the rest.

If you think that all employees are completely altruistic all the time and would never take an action that personally benefits them at the cost of their colleagues, I guess you can stop here.

But if you have observed that people sometimes behave selfishly and dishonestly, read on.

Let's assume unethical behavior is evenly distributed across all groups. Protected classes have more opportunities to exploit the laws precisely because they have laws protecting them.

This means that some employees come with higher implicit total costs than others. For example:

- Women as a group spend fewer hours in paid work than men on average. This is because they spend more time on unpaid family-related tasks and because women have traditionally taken more maternity leave than men paternity leave. A pay gap that relates to fewer hours worked is still unequal pay on its face, however, which gives room to complaints.

- Employees respond differently to adverse employment decisions in my experience. Some accept they could do better and try to improve. Others claim any bad outcome must be the result of discrimination and complain accordingly. No company fires a protected-class employee without carefully considering the risk of a lawsuit.

- A similar calculation occurs on the part of employers considering adverse actions against over 40-year-old employees. Although it is relatively easy to avoid an age discrimination claim, doing so requires advance planning and limits companies' flexibility. Hence, over-40 employees have a relatively higher cost from this perspective as well.

If new employees, women, historically underrepresented minorities, and everyone over 40 are relatively riskier and hence more expensive, who does that leave?

Hypothesis 4 — The sweet spot consists of white men in their 30s who do not otherwise fall in a protected class.

They have been with the company for 5–10 years. By then you know the cultural fit is good. If employees have lasted that long, they usually navigate the workplace well and so are less likely to complain.

They also have enough experience to be productive at their jobs but have not had decades of annual salary increases that make them expensive just with the passage of time.

Considering each of the factors above, white men in their 30s appear to be the employees least likely to complain and cause friction for their companies.

Some of you will be saying, "That's right, and it's because *they have the least to complain about.*" That may be entirely true.

But if white men complain less on average, it could also be because they have fewer laws protecting them. That is, they are among the only groups it is safe to openly discriminate against.

Either way, they generate lower total costs for their employers.

Should you take any of this as an argument in favor of hiring more white men? Not at all.

It is an observation that promoting diversity comes with a cost to companies because of the laws that favor protected classes and the fact that some individuals will seek to exploit those laws.

This may help explain why it has taken longer to develop diverse workforces than everyone expected considering the obvious social and reputation benefits to doing so.

Ignoring financial incentives won't work

Considering all this, can we do anything to improve the situation?

One option is to keep raising the social costs on companies that do not promote diversity quickly enough. This makes it easier for companies to justify paying overall higher costs to compensate for occasional bad actors.

We may also consider raising the costs on those individuals who make false claims because they artificially raise the costs of the entire protected class.

What probably won't work is ignoring companies' financial incentives when they evaluate how expensive different employees actually are.

Be well.

Chapter Thirteen

Why Aren't More Pharma Companies Nonprofits?

The shareholder model is absurdly counterproductive in the case of pharma companies

This essay is about the power of incentives. When you look past the surface of things to the incentives that drive behavior, you sometimes find surprising things.

Full disclosure: I believe in the shareholder model of capitalism and the theory that companies pursuing their own long-term profit will drive the maximum benefits not just to shareholders but to society as a whole.

I say this despite having worked for more than a decade on sustainability topics and also believing strongly in the benefits of a broad environmental, social, and governance (ESG) strategy.

Having run a global sustainability program, I am aware of the growing chorus of calls for companies to discard the idea of shareholder primacy as having long since served its purpose.

The stakeholder framework's fatal flaw

My principal objection to stakeholder capitalism is that we have yet to identify a consistent framework for choosing priorities among competing stakeholders.

A company has many stakeholders, all of whom rightly believe their concerns are paramount. Stakeholders respond to the competition by ratcheting up the pressure on companies to pay attention to their issue.

The public pressure leads to the misallocation of resources in which companies waste money in areas where they do not have the greatest potential impact.

Shareholder primacy isn't perfect either

I have come to understand two necessary modifications to my belief in the fundamental soundness of shareholder capitalism.

First, we can solve the problems of the stakeholder model by allowing companies to determine in good faith their unique opportunities for the greatest stakeholder impact.

What would happen if we allowed those companies who genuinely want to make positive contributions to determine freely where and how they would do so? I expect we would see much better performance on those metrics.

True, not always in those areas that some stakeholders would prefer. But I ask you what's better in the long run? Second-rate forced compliance on topics the company doesn't fundamentally agree are important, or enthusiastic all-in commitments on selected topics?

Second, some types of business are ill-suited for the shareholder model. The reason is the very thing that makes the shareholder model so effective: incentives.

The normal incentive is for companies to grow their long-term profits, which accrue to the benefit of many stakeholders, including shareholders. The emphasis on the long term is what keeps companies from committing harm to certain stakeholders.

What opponents of capitalism conveniently ignore is that no company is successful over the long term that breaks the law, underpays employees, squeezes suppliers, or cheats customers.

The mechanisms are not perfect, and we see many temporary exceptions that outrage us, but it is hard to argue with the improvements in much of humanity's quality of life that have been brought about by modern capitalism.

Mismatched incentives are a source of great mischief

That said, is it possible for a company's good faith successful pursuit of long-term profitability to create incentives that are harmful for their customers and for society as a whole?

The staggering cost of healthcare in the United States combined with relatively poor outcomes strongly suggests this is so, at least for some market participants.

Healthcare costs have been steadily increasing such that Americans now pay more than people in any other country for their care. But Americans are not getting healthier. For evidence, we can look at developments in life expectancy, preventable years of life lost, and the leading causes of death.

Here's the mismatch between pharmaceutical companies' incentives and their customers' incentives:

- Pharma companies wish to have proprietary drugs approved so they can exclusively sell them to patients for the greatest profit.

- Customers wish to be healthy and well.

- Drug trials are designed to prove the efficacy of a drug compared to not taking the drug. The trials are *not designed* to prove the efficacy of that drug compared to other interventions, including non-pharmacological inventions.

- As a result, the US Food and Drug Administration (FDA) approves many drugs for use *without any evidence that they provide the best outcome for patients (i.e., health and wellness).*

Perhaps a diabetes drug does reduce the risk of heart complications in one out of several hundred patients. That small benefit may be enough to warrant approval of that drug to treat patients.

But nowhere must the pharma company describe or even mention that a program of diet and exercise might be vastly more effective at treating both diabetes and cardiovascular risk.

What kinds of patients are the ideal customers for pharma companies? Those who never or only sparingly take medications in favor of lifestyle interventions? Or those who become lifelong customers of a drug?

The patient's desire to become healthy cuts directly against the pharma company's interest in selling its medications to forever patients.

It's not the employees' fault, but can't we do better?

Now I must point out a great irony. I think the vast majority of employees who work for pharma companies are honest and well-meaning and believe they are making positive contributions to society.

Everyone I know who ever worked for a pharma company expressed personal satisfaction at the strong social benefit they presumed their company delivered.

Almost no one is alert to the fact that, in this special case, their company's incentives are grossly misaligned with their stated values.

Would today's pharma companies be just as effective if they were organized as not-for-profit companies? If we assume employees are genuine in their desire to help cure disease and be a positive force in society, and I do believe this, I see no reason why not.

In contrast, I see every reason why the shareholder model is counterproductive in the case of pharma companies, which leaves me with today's question:

Why aren't more pharma companies nonprofits?

I genuinely have no answer. Let me know if you think you do.

Be well.

Chapter Fourteen

Corporations Are People Too

The blanket criticisms of corporations are not based in fact, but when a majority of the public believes the bad press, we better watch out

E ffective in-house counsel help their companies address many risks facing their businesses. Today, a key risk is societal doubt about the benefits of corporations themselves.

If we want our companies to be free to pursue business without intrusive regulation, then we need to think carefully about corporate reputations. In-house lawyers can play a critical role in this evaluation.

"Greedy corporations!" We hear this so often it is almost a reflexive response.

Or how about, "All corporations are evil," a Hollywood refrain so common it has led to many young people believing it as a matter of fact.

Certainly, executives of large companies are inherently suspect, the original "fat cats," paying themselves obscene amounts of money.

If you work for a large company, it is easy to dismiss these complaints. After all, you, personally, are a good person, and just about everyone you work with is as well.

You see occasional incompetence, true, perhaps a touch of arrogance, but certainly no evil. Of the many thousands of corporations, a tiny number end up committing malfeasance.

Because of this, it is typically only people who don't work for large companies who hold such derogatory views of them.

The good and the bad of corporations

What we sometimes underestimate, however, is how many people do not work for large companies. This makes our ignoring the phenomenon risky.

We may know that the blanket criticisms of corporations are not based on fact, but when a majority of the public believes the bad press, we better watch out.

And it is not just investment banks, oil companies, or cigarette manufacturers. Politicians and the media focus a roving spotlight on the particular villains of the day, but no one is safe from their harsh gaze.

The scope of environmental, social, and governance (ESG) stakeholder interests is so broad that virtually every corporation may fall victim to a negative influence campaign at some point.

Critics and defenders

Is there anyone who will speak out on behalf of corporations?

Each individual company has a strong incentive to stay silent. Why draw attention to yourself? Better to be quiet and hope that the news cycle will turn to another victim.

Milton Friedman spoke eloquently in 1970 about the social responsibility of business. His point then was that businesses brought about the greatest good for society when they focused on increasing their profit.

Academics and advocates are questioning the past five decades of shareholder primacy in the stakeholder v. shareholder debate.

But this debate glosses over the most important point about the role of corporations: Far from being greedy or evil, corporations have been a steady source of significant good in society.

When did we all lose the script?

Corporations are strongholds

One of the most amazing features of corporations is their potential for indefinite life. This is because while a corporation is comprised of the people who work for it at any given moment, it has a separate, independent existence.

For legal purposes, corporations are people too. The individuals who serve in various functions come and go, but the corporation itself continues on.

I worked for a company with a more than 100-year history. No one involved at the time our company was formed is alive today.

Of course, the company evolved over this time. But the company still is involved in recognizably the same business, selling products meeting a similar need, albeit with vastly improved technology and performance.

I sometimes marveled at how many people worked at my company over the years. How many livelihoods we supported, and how much influence our products had on the world.

Yes, corporations are people too, and what people they are! Capable of coordinating the collective efforts of tens and thousands of people across decades and centuries.

Corporations preserve humankind's know-how and encourage steady improvements in products and services. This has brought untold prosperity and better living conditions to many millions of people across the world.

In most other areas of life, we celebrate the power of collective human action:

- from a simple employee union that brings negotiation power to a group of individuals,

- to massive research efforts (think of the remarkable effort to develop COVID vaccines in record time),

- to even greater scientific feats of human achievement, such as the moon landings or the deployment of the James Webb Space Telescope.

Rights and the Rule of Law

But also on the individual level, Western society has thrived on the principle of protection of individual rights.

We allow people to pursue their self-interest unreservedly, subject only to operating within the law.

We incentivize risky exploration by allowing people to reap the benefit of their individual efforts. Many ventures fail, but when an individual succeeds, they can become wildly successful.

Allowing and encouraging people to pursue their self-interest benefits all of society.

The rule of law undergirds this system: If you play within the rules, society will protect your person and your property.

There is nothing more fundamental than protecting personal property from predation by other people or the government itself. What you accumulate through your efforts belongs to you.

If corporations are people too, what possible reason can justify changing the rules to apply, for example, an "excess profits" tax?

What undermining of the rule of law warrants telling successful people that, although they played by the rules of the game, they have been too successful?

For every corporation you secretly cheered getting grilled by a grandstanding member of US Congress remember this: It's not just corporations that are people. You are too.

What we do to corporations can just as easily be done to us.

Be well.

Chapter Fifteen

Can Anything Save Corporations' Tainted Image?

In the last 25 years, the number of US public companies has dropped by half

M any in society question whether corporations provide sufficient benefit for the supposed harm they cause.

If we want our companies to be free to pursue business without intrusive regulation, we need to think carefully about corporate reputations. In-house lawyers can play a critical role in this evaluation.

Although there have been exceptionally bad actors, corporations' legacy is, on balance, overwhelmingly positive. In the previous essay, I talked about how corporations have contributed to the flourishing of humankind.

I explore here what it is that makes corporations so deeply unsympathetic in the public eye today. And as importantly, whether there is anything corporations can do to turn public sympathy to their side once more.

I think we can chalk corporations' bad image up to two things: Scope of influence and confirmation bias. Here's what I mean.

They've gotten bigger and bigger

Because of global networks, large corporations have been getting larger, particularly technology companies.

It is easier for an incumbent to buy a small company and incorporate their novel technology than it is to compete with them. The more technologies and services a company incorporates into its offerings, the more valuable it becomes to consumers.

For their part, smaller companies have every incentive to sell to larger competitors. There is no guarantee they'll succeed on their own and being a public company today is burdensome.

Society puts substantial regulations on companies for fear that the bad acts of a few will become the norm for all. Ironically, this heavy-handed approach has led to ever fewer companies either choosing to go public or remaining independent.

In the last 25 years, the number of US public companies has dropped by half. At the same time, our economies have grown, which means that fewer companies are dividing up ever-increasing markets.

Hence, companies' scope of influence on our lives has increased visibly.

The bad rap is often exaggerated

This enhanced influence would be unproblematic but for the second point: Confirmation bias.

We are now primed to expect bad behavior from corporations because of prominent examples that politicians and pundits make sure are publicly exposed.

When you expect bad behavior, any example, no matter how isolated, will reinforce your belief and confirm your suspicions.

Thus, a tiny number of incidents has led to overblown concerns. To understand the point, you need only consider the many people who are scared to fly but think nothing of hopping in their cars.

They need to do more than good deeds

What can corporations do? Having attained the reputation as the schoolyard bully or worse, it will not help for corporations to point out their many good deeds.

A year of patient benevolence is undone by pushing down one kid in the playground and taking their lunch money.

I think of this when I read companies' sustainability reports. Page after page of good deeds, which have no effect on the reader, other than for some to suspect the company of greenwashing.

Know why corporations are important

The reason recitations of good deeds won't help is because society no longer considers the net positive impact corporations have had on society in the past two centuries.

Partly this is a matter of short-termism, as in, "What have you done for me lately?"

Partly it is a matter of being spoiled by good times. We don't personally remember when our quality of life was materially worse and when products and services from household-name corporations changed all that.

Lastly as noted above, we are primed to think corporations are filled with selfish, bad actors, and so extrapolate the acts of a few to all.

Well, what about pointing out what happens in countries when private enterprise is squelched, and the government steps in to provide basic goods and services?

Cuba, Venezuela, and North Korea are clear warning signals for tampering with individual incentives. Surely a reminder of this would bring an ungrateful public around, right?

Sadly, this hope is also misguided. People do not reliably learn from history; they rarely learn from their own experiences and almost never from those of others.

Because of, again, confirmation bias, such as: "I believe corporations are evil and their function would be better performed by the central government. Thus, any evidence to the contrary I simply dismiss. Cuba and Venezuela are a mess, true. But if we were running the show, we would avoid their obvious problems."

Become a benefit corporation

No, corporations need a radical change of frame. Tinkering around the edges of society's malcontent with a feel-good story in your next corporate responsibility report won't do.

I suggest that for corporations to survive for the next 50 years in a recognizable form, they need to reframe themselves as *operating primarily for the benefit of society*.

Have shareholders vote on converting the company to a benefit corporation. Nothing short of this will snap a jaded public out of its negative view.

Societal benefit looks different today than when Milton Friedman advocated for shareholder primacy.

- Then, shareholders were expected to take net profits and reinvest them in further productive enterprises.

- Today, shareholders have reaped decades of gain from companies' remarkable success and, considering overall wealth, further gains only go to fund lavish excesses.

If shareholders of the largest companies in the world voted to become or similar according to the country's law, individuals would believe companies once again represented a force for good in society.

Short of that, don't hold your breath.

Be well.

PS — If this sounds too drastic to you, don't worry: Companies and shareholders also suffer from confirmation bias, which means they will convince themselves that the status quo is just fine.

Chapter Sixteen

Do You Have Skin in the Game?

Look for where one party has greater upside than downside or a potential gain with little cost and you will find the sources of bad behavior

S pending time with colleagues working at other companies gave me an unexpected benefit.

I realized my fellow in-house colleagues were facing all the same problems as me. No one had a perfect solution to their problems, and we were all muddling along doing the best we could.

In fact, some colleagues had it far worse than me: those whose companies sold products to end consumers, so-called B-to-C companies.

It seems like not a week went by when I didn't say to myself, "Thank goodness you don't have to deal with the individual public as customers." Prompted, of course, by some idiot suing a consumer goods company on transparently frivolous grounds.

Or even when it appeared there might be a sliver of merit, then suing for such inflated amounts that I could never forget where the phrase "deep pockets" came from.

And this was years before the whole environmental, social, and governance (ESG) movement became front-page news. These same companies that had widespread brand recognition were natural targets for the early activists.

- A shareholder proposal at Coke or Nestlé got you much more publicity simply because everyone recognizes the name of your company.

- Still today, the nature of your customer and shareholder base is a great predictor of whether and what types of shareholder proposals will pop up during proxy season.

Working for a B-to-B company that nobody in the public had any reason to know or care about was a great advantage. Yes, my in-house friends at Starbucks and McDonald's ran out of business cards at every get-together. But I read the headlines like everyone else and consoled myself that it is better to be unseen than in the spotlight, at least if you're in-house counsel.

We had our share of issues, no doubt. Many of our customers were big, powerful companies, much more capable of vigorously defending their interests than any individual consumer.

And because these customers bought large amounts of products, when something went wrong, it was almost always worth pursuing.

The joy of just doing business

Here's the lovely thing about B-to-B businesses: Neither companies nor their business customers have any incentive to push frivolous lawsuits. We just want to do business on reasonable terms.

We typically have long business relationships and want to preserve the relationship. So when a problem arises, it is in both our interests to find a quick, fair solution.

When a business customer decides to sue a supplier, the customer pays for it in the long run.

What all this means is that B-to-B companies' and customers' incentives are aligned. We want to make the best possible products and sell them for a fair price. Customers want to buy the best products for a fair price.

Lawsuit-happy businesses are another matter

Now consider the B-to-C relationship.

When you buy a treat from Nestlé or Kraft, you are not forming a meaningful, lifelong relationship with either company.

But if you chip a tooth snacking on a cracker, some plaintiff's lawyer will slither out and tell you that you can get thousands of dollars. And best of all, it won't cost you a thing!

In this case, your incentives are not aligned with the company's and are rather exactly opposed. You have no downside risk (also known as "skin in the game") because you suffer no costs if you lose. It's all upside to you.

Your lawyer similarly has almost no skin in the game. True, they need to file a lawsuit, but this is something they've done many times before. They simply change the plaintiff's name on their standard form complaint, update their outrageously overbroad list of requested discovery subjects and topics, and the costs and burdens shift to the company.

Your lawyer knows that the cost of defending even frivolous lawsuits is so high that companies make the economically rational choice to settle many of them. What is a nuisance settlement for *Nestlé* is bread and butter to your lawyer: 40 percent of US$30,000 for doing little more than printing off a copy of a standard complaint is easy money. So it's all upside to your lawyer as well.

Playing the incentive game

This mismatch of incentives explains a great deal of what in-house lawyers do. Look for where one party has greater upside than downside or a potential gain with little cost and you will find the sources of bad behavior.

Let's assume salespeople are compensated based on the volume of new business they bring in. Will they care as much about the terms of the contract as they will landing a new customer? You know the answer.

How to identify your greatest risks

Looking at who has skin in the game helps you identify your greatest compliance risks.

Consider how material are the risks that an individual can cause by their actions. No matter what type of company you work for, this analysis usually leads you to the conclusion that senior management creates your greatest exposure.

Senior management has tremendous upside, which encourages them to take risks. They are often well-insulated against downside risk. Yes, they may be dinged on their cash incentive for one year, but their long-term equity incentives still pay off handsomely. Thus, they have insufficient skin in the game.

The time in-house counsel spend rolling out compliance programs to every employee worldwide is largely for show. If we're honest, it's partly a distraction by management to deflect attention from their own incentives for mischief.

In-house counsel's incentives are usually properly aligned with the company's. That is, we don't want compliance problems and we feel the consequences when they occur.

Looking at your compliance program, ask yourself this question: How much time do you spend on window-dressing versus designing incentives tailored to your greatest risks?

Be well.

Chapter Seventeen

Lawmakers Need a Hippocratic Oath

Passing new laws and regulations without sufficiently considering the likely but unwanted adverse consequences is foolish and risky

I magine a world where your performance was measured, not by outcomes, but simply by your intentions.

Boss: "Hi Sam, come on in. So, annual performance evaluation time already, huh?"

You: "Yes, Pat, can't wait! It was a great year."

Boss: "Hmm, we'll talk about that. I saw on your self-evaluation you gave yourself a 110 percent rating across the board."

You: "Sure did! I took that goal of implementing a compliance program in Europe, and I ran with it. Why, I had the most amazing project plan you've ever seen."

"Sam, are you forgetting we got sued by the EU Antitrust Commission for starting up an illegal cartel with our three biggest competitors? I have to testify in Brussels next month!"

"Pat, Pat, let's stay focused. On paper, I designed a perfect program. I even called it the Perfect Compliance Program. Why, the training videos alone won awards for most innovative use of Claymation."

"Oh, don't mention those videos to me. Everywhere we showed them management ended up engaging in more *illegal behavior, not less. It seems like your examples only inspired them to find more ways to bend the law."*

"That's certainly not my fault. I was only following best practices. And remember, we had that consultant come in and tell us our program ticked all the boxes? No, my intentions were pure."

"Since when do we measure performance by intentions, Sam?"

In the business world, the answer is a clear "never." But when it comes to our politicians and regulators, we all seem to stop at good intentions. Why do I say this? It is because I spent decades managing the unintended consequences of laws passed with the best of intentions.

Policymaking can be a waste of time

Grandstanding lawmakers and overworked regulators slap a rule in place with a catchy title like the Anti-Money Laundering Act. "See, it's got 'Anti' right in the title; we're taking a stand against criminals." Never mind that the consequences of the law's reporting requirements are that honest companies are now routinely hounded by their banking partners to declare ever more detailed chains of beneficial owners with no appreciable effect on actual money launderers.

Laws can do worse than simply not achieve their goals

They can lead to the exact opposite outcome than was intended. Consider the cautionary tale of attempts to rein in executive compensation.

One early idea was to limit executive compensation by forbidding companies from deducting pay that exceeded US$1 million. But the law allowed companies to deduct "performance-based compensation" approved by shareholders. The result (predictable in hindsight) was public companies adopting stock option plans and an explosion in equity-based compensation.

Then regulators decided they would require companies to publicly disclose their compensation in painful detail. Even if executives themselves were unashamed, the thinking went, shareholders seeing the details would curtail the worst excesses.

The result was again exactly the opposite of what was intended. How so? Compensation committees benchmark executive pay against peer companies. Where previously there were gray areas and some guesswork, the details became clear to all. Once-missed perks were now added to the calculus.

Worse, the sincere belief that your executives are better than average supports paying above the median. But when everyone does this, the median itself steadily rises. While performance is not notably different, pay has risen steadily year-on-year for decades.

Passing new laws and regulations without sufficiently considering the likely but unwanted adverse consequences is foolish and risky.

So why do we keep doing it? For lawmakers the answer is clear: Their incentive is always to take action, and they have no skin in the game, i.e., they suffer no consequence for bad laws.

Why do we allow bad policy?

Why does the voting public accept repeated poor performance? After all, we are affected by poorly designed laws and grapple with unintended consequences all the time. Is it because we can't see a better way? I can think of at least three alternatives:

1. **No new laws**. At least prevent lawmakers from making things worse. I welcome gridlock for this very reason. But there are real problems we need to address as a society, so we do want effective lawmaking.

2. **Sunset all new laws**. Let lawmakers pass new laws, but build in a review mechanism. That is, lawmakers must revisit the law's performance after some period, say 10 years, and decide whether to scrap it, keep it, or amend it in light of unintended consequences.

3. **Give lawmakers skin in the game**. Just like executives now must stand behind the company's financials, make politicians personally responsible for the laws they adopt. An easy first step would be making sure lawmakers are subject to the same rules as the general public, which is surprisingly often not the case. Then let's make lawmakers sign up to a modified Hippocratic Oath.

You probably heard an excerpt of the Hippocratic Oath as being "first do no harm." The longer excerpt is actually "I will abstain from all intentional wrong-doing and harm."

Intentional harm includes the reasonably foreseeable consequences of your actions. Just because you didn't want something to happen, you are still responsible if a reasonable person could anticipate that it will happen.

With all this in mind, the Lawmakers' Oath would read as follows:

> I will ensure that the intended benefits of all laws I propose are not outweighed by both anticipated harms *and* probable but unintended effects. I will regularly assess the real world actual benefits *and* harms to evaluate the performance of the laws and adjust accordingly.

I don't expect lawmakers to do much better right away. But the Lawmakers' Oath would give voters a way to objectively measure their performance. That seems like a good start to me.

Be well.

Chapter Eighteen

I'm a Better Manager Now that I'm Out of the Job

It takes quiet time and reflection to tease out meaningful learnings from our chaotic days

When you share your thoughts publicly, you wonder how people will react. Will they see what you've written, do they agree with your ideas? Perhaps most importantly, for me at least, will anything you've said be helpful to them in their lives?

I love writing these Career Paths essays. It helps me shape my intuitions, feelings, and more or less well-founded practices into tangible advice. I also appreciate the reach that publishing gives me, as well as the opportunity to interact with readers.

So it was that I found myself responding to a commenter on an earlier article. I noted that I wasn't always able to give good advice in a timely way when I was in my management role and that I was happy to do so now.

Quiet, strategic thought time can make you great

We're busy at work, and we have many demands on our time. I've found it takes quiet time and reflection to tease out meaningful learnings from our chaotic days.

While working, I knew the importance of carving out time for strategic thinking. I told my team that regularly making time for strategic thought was one of the things that distinguished great in-house counsel from merely good ones.

So we devoted time to strategy. But it was almost always business strategy, or rather legal strategy in pursuit of business goals. Only now with some time and distance from my general counsel role do I see some pretty big gaps in where I spent my time and where I might have invested more time.

Lessons learned later in life

I learned a lot over the years about managing a team and being effective. But I wasn't always effective at consolidating those lessons and then sharing them with my colleagues.

I find myself saying often these days, "Boy, I wish I had spent more time exploring this idea with my team when I was working!" I just didn't have the time because of the press of daily work. Honestly, I don't think any active manager has the time for considered reflection on many non-core topics.

When I look at how much time I invest now in organizing my thoughts and summarizing ideas, I am alternatively amazed and depressed. I think I'm pretty efficient, and I can write quickly and well. But many are the days that I look up to find 10 hours have passed with my face still lit by a screen and my hands poised over a keyboard.

To be fair, I am writing about many topics beyond those here in Career Paths. Stoic philosophy and how to live a good life. Economics, politics, and psychology. Junk science and the march of human progress. And no one is holding my feet to the fire.

Writing down interesting ideas engages me, as does the idea of helping other people in a way that I would have appreciated when I was younger.

My point is simply this: Getting better at anything takes time, practice, and reflection. Although most of us learn to implement well by necessity, we can do so comfortably without also developing a philosophy or working model that explains and guides our actions. The bigger picture, if you will, comes only upon reflection.

With this in mind, here's another thing I can tell you was a great use of my time when I was working, even though many consider it non-core: Reading widely. It was because I religiously read professional journals that I was able to keep up on so many topics.

Few people are experts on lots of topics. The good news is we don't have to be. All you need is access to a few good experts on topics that interest you.

If I'm a better manager now that I'm out of the job of managing, I hope I can help you be a better manager now by sharing with you my learnings. What you do with those learnings is up to you.

Be well.

Chapter Nineteen

What the Heck Were They Thinking?

Although it's true we sometimes learn from our own mistakes, it's considerably less embarrassing to use other people's screwups for our teachable moments

I 'm a little tired of "best of" awards, truth be told. In my professional life, not a week went by without some law firm being celebrated for an accolade.

In-house counsel seem to do fewer, but we still hand out awards like clockwork such as for best law departments, GCs of the year, and the ACC Top 10 30-Somethings (of which I served as a judge). There are hundreds and hundreds of them.

Now, it's not that the law firms, departments, and individual lawyers who are nominated and who win these awards aren't awesome. They usually are pretty great and deserving of recognition.

The award serves as a temporary boost to the ego, provides a little thrill of recognition, can get you introduced to folks you'd like to know, looks good on your resume, and reassures you that you haven't given up a large chunk of your waking hours for nothing.

The thing is, there's not a great deal awards can teach us. In fact, that a majority of votes went to Person X at Firm Y could mean one of several things.

- Maybe voting was light that year and the marketing department did a great job getting their friends' friends to vote.

- Maybe the judges were lazy or incompetent.

- Or maybe the donation the firm made to the voting committee's favorite charity wasn't completely coincidental.

But let's take even the best assumption, i.e., the winner is a great lawyer who delights their clients. OK, what does that do for me? How does it help me provide a better service?

I'd rather know what the worst lawyers did

I'll tell you what would be much more valuable to know: Who are the worst lawyers and what did they do that made them stand out?

Flagrant public mistakes can provide great learning experiences. Although it's true we sometimes learn from our own mistakes, it's considerably less embarrassing to use other people's screwups for our teachable moments.

You might be surprised to hear there are far fewer lists nominating "the worst lawyer of the year" or "the biggest legal screwups of the decade." Or maybe you're not surprised. Lawyers are a sue-happy group, come to think of it. Probably not a good idea to go around seeking nominations for your new "worst lawyer" list, although I bet you could get some new advertisers to buy space in your award publication.

The closest analogy I can think of are periodic lists compiled by law firms of the largest fines and settlements companies paid to resolve enforcement actions.

These penalties are the result of sometimes epic misconduct and mismanagement, but it is rare for individuals to be singled out. In just the last few years, each of Airbus, Petrobas, Ericsson, and Telia coughed up more than a billion dollars in fine for paying bribes. Do you know any of the involved parties' names?

It would be really interesting to know what management was thinking in these companies. You don't get to problems that big without senior management malfeasance:

- Either their direct involvement, or

- They knew about it and didn't stop it, or

- They didn't know but should have known.

The thought process in all three cases would be fascinating to understand. Why did they make the decisions they did? Would we have been tempted to make the same decisions?

The annual "What Were They Thinking" Awards

Because we should be open to continuous improvement from wherever inspiration strikes, I propose we establish an annual "What Were They Thinking?" list for counsel of companies and institutions that experience public crises.

No need to crown an overall winner, and no need to pour salt on the wounds by referring to anything so rude as the "worst lawyers."

And if we're honest, we should demonstrate humility when judging others. What seems like an obvious mistake after a crisis has unfolded was in all likelihood anything but clear at the time. We're talking about smart, accomplished, often well-meaning people who were doing their absolute best in difficult circumstances, not hacks or crooks.

We could use these criteria for counsel's potential inclusion on the list:

- A deliberate decision (or lack of a decision) leading to significant corporate harm. In other words, there has to be one or more avoidable moments we can second-guess.

- The harm must make its way into the public eye. Lots of bad stuff happens that we never hear about. This isn't about surfacing companies' private business.

- Legal counsel either made the decision or was closely involved with those that did and so should have been able to influence the decision.

With this in mind, I quickly came up with the following candidates:

- Disney's counsel in letting the CEO say the company would explicitly fight to overturn a democratically adopted law in the State of Florida that had broad public support.

- Twitter's counsel for suppressing the news about Hunter Biden's laptop two weeks before the presidential election, making it appear as if they were choosing sides on a topic of clear national relevance.

- Boeing's counsel for allowing a circumstance to arise where safety officials say they felt their voices were overridden by business concerns.

- The Motion Picture Academy's counsel on thinking that a 10-year suspension for Will Smith attending the Academy Awards was appropriate while allowing him to retain his award.

Politics is so heated that I have great sympathy for any company that makes a misstep, egregious though they may be. Sometimes the pressure to take a stand is overwhelming. And I would bet there are a lot of companies whose safety officials feel underappreciated and underfunded. The slap and its consequences may not seem to reflect obviously poor decision-making to you.

So I'll offer up one more candidate for the "What Were They Thinking" nominations —

- Credit Suisse's counsel for their inability to control either CS's internal compliance culture or the flow of damaging information to the press. Any company can be hit by a scandal, and follow-on scandals are not that rare. After all, once authorities give you a good looking-over, they are more likely to find more troublesome things. But if your company makes global headlines month after month for a string of scandals over a multi-year period, something's gone terribly wrong.

I'd be interested to know who you think should make the list.

Be well.

PS — When I wrote this, Credit Suisse had yet to collapse and be taken over by its archrival UBS. I felt vindicated, but it turns out no one likes the bearer of bad news, especially if they turn out to be prescient.

Chapter Twenty

Failure Hidden in Plain Sight

Women are well-represented in the law, or so it seems. Digging deeper reveals some shocking gaps

I n-house lawyers are a bit of a secret weapon for companies, but not in the way you may be thinking. Sure, we keep the wheels of commerce rolling smoothly, manage a slew of business risks, and are essential allies in a crisis. What HR teams and management secretly love, however, is how much in-house lawyers contribute to companies' diversity efforts.

Where can we find a group that not only is majority-comprised of women but has excellent management representation, even frequently in executive management? The legal team is exemplary at many companies.*

The reasons for in-house legal teams' outperformance no doubt include our genuine commitment to diversity. But we also benefit from two powerful environmental factors: ample supply and weak competition.

I'll describe both factors and why our very success is contributing to an ugly distortion in the broader legal community. I'll end with a concrete recommendation about what in-house legal teams can do to help move towards balance.

Supply: A rich palette of talent to choose from

Law school is the ultimate egalitarian endeavor. At least as it concerns gender parity, women and men have been enrolling in law school in equal numbers for decades. Women enrollees have started outpacing men every year starting in 2016.

What this means is that when in-house legal teams need to hire new lawyers, we are spoiled for choice, certainly compared to many professions.

For reasons I'll explain in a moment, an even greater proportion of female lawyers than law school graduates want to work in-house. What's going on, you wonder, and where's the failure I'm hinting at?

Competition: Why is in-house practice desirable?

Before we congratulate ourselves on being so wonderful, consider that it might not be us so much as the wretched competition.

According to ABA statistics, more than half of law school graduates enter private practice upon leaving law school. Just about 10 percent start by working in-house. That certainly doesn't look like in-house teams have any recruiting advantage.

But what happens each year after lawyers start to work? A certain percentage leave their law firms and look to move in-house. That reliable recurrence is what concerns us today.

The depressing truth: Law firms are failing on a grand scale

When I say law firms are failing, I mean they're failing to create an environment in which women thrive and move into more senior roles. Consider this:

- Women constitute not quite half (47 percent) of all associates at law firms.

- Women represent 32 percent of all non-equity partners.

- Just 22 percent of law firm equity partners are women.

From starting in the majority as junior associates, women steadily leave law firms at greater rates than men and are significantly underrepresented in management. Not only that, but male partners have substantially higher average compensation than women partners.

If you ask them, everyone involved will tell you they're unhappy about this. The women for certain, as we'll see in a moment, but the men leading law firms as well.

In what ways do law firms underperform?

The results of detailed inquiries into the law firm experience are sobering (from the ABA Profile of the Legal Profession 2022): In each of the following categories, vastly more women than men missed out on a desirable assignment, were denied a salary increase or bonus, were denied or overlooked for advancement or promotion, or were perceived as less committed to their career. Women experienced a lack of access to business development opportunities, were mistaken for lower-level employees, and experienced demeaning comments, stories, or jokes.

According to the same ABA study, the three top reasons women say they leave law firms are because of caretaking commitments, stress at work, and the emphasis on marketing or originating business.

Well, there you have it. Suddenly it becomes clear why in-house practice looks so attractive. We offer flexibility and part-time work, we are careful to acknowledge and mitigate stressful conditions, and our lawyers have no pressure to originate business.

Can in-house lawyers help solve law firms' problems?

Let's assume law firms are making genuine efforts to stem the loss of so many talented women. Whatever they're doing is not working.

No matter how good one's intentions are, perceptions form reality. The statistics about women's daily experiences show what those perceptions are, and they're not good.

A lot of well-meaning people have spent a lot of time both thinking about this and trying to improve. It would be arrogant of us to assume we know their motives or how to create better outcomes.

But we do know that incentives drive behavior. If today's behaviors are not driving the desired outcomes, then the incentives are not sufficiently aligned. It is thus on the incentive side where in-house counsel may play a constructive role.

Because I don't think anyone has an easy fix, it's likely counter-productive for us to try to mandate an outcome. Individually we don't have the leverage and such requests are adjacent to our core work priorities.

Perhaps we can create greater incentives by reminding law firms this issue is important to us. How? *Just ask them about it.* That is much easier and relatively non-controversial.

If the majority of a firm's clients are routinely asking about diversity, law firm management would have a new incentive to keep trying.

Three questions in-house teams could ask their outside counsel

How about once a year we simply ask our law firms these questions:

1. What are the current diversity statistics for your firm as a whole? How do these compare to the prior two years?

2. What are the diversity details of the lawyers currently working on our engagement?

3. Please describe any commitment to improve your diversity performance you have made. How have your prior commitments been implemented?

Be careful what you wish for

Note that if we're successful in moving the law firm needle, we're going to make it harder to recruit lawyers to our in-house teams from private practice.

Rather than having a job that sells itself because the competition is terrible, we'll have to convince potential hires how wonderful we are. I am confident we're up to the challenge.

Be well.

* While this discussion cites data from the US legal market, I've observed similar trends in other markets, including in Europe and India.

Chapter Twenty-One

Corporate Greed Should Be Low on Our List of Worries

A thought experiment on what would happen if we tried to promote "fairness" by eliminating "greed." Beware! You may come away feeling differently

Are corporations greedy? I notice that people use the word "greed" carelessly in two misleading ways. First, they imply that greed is unnatural and immoral. And second, they behave as if greed afflicts only one party to a transaction.

What is greed? Looking beyond the quick answer

Greed is, in fact, a completely natural impulse. Let's say you're holding a garage sale: You've got your front yard filled with unneeded toys, sports equipment, and clothing. Two people are interested in your old bike.

- One says they'll pay you US$100 and the other says they'll pay you US$200.

- Are you greedy if you take the US$200? Or are you simply behaving rationally?

Assuming that transactions between market participants are unforced (that is, consensual on both sides), can it be immoral to allow a transaction to take place exactly as both parties wish?

Before you decide on the morality of market transactions, consider the second point: Which of us is the greedy one? We assume it is the seller who is the greedy party: Greedy corporations raising prices and taking advantage of consumers. But what about the buyers?

If one person at your garage sale bidding on your bike earns twice as much as the other person, and can comfortably pay more, are they greedy for using their superior earnings to their advantage? To give another example, are the young professionals moving to your town and bidding up home prices greedy because they can pay more?

Take two persons earning the same amount of money but placing different values on things. Person A likes to travel to new places and places a premium on their vacations. They could live in a small apartment and be happy. Person B loves to be at home and wants a house with a yard.

When these two want to book a flight, Person A is willing to pay considerably more of their income to get the flight they want. When it comes to their housing, Person B is willing to pay more of their income to get the home they want.

Is Person A greedy? Are they both greedy? Or do their decisions merely reflect different values and choices?

If you believe a seller is greedy for preferring to receive more money instead of less money, by the same logic, a buyer is greedy for being willing to pay more than another bidder to get what they want.

Subjective and arbitrary standards, including "fairness"

Right now, you might be feeling uncomfortable with your understanding of greed, and for good reason. When we consider either the seller or the buyer to be greedy, a problem arises, because we compare the actual transaction with a hypothetical one that we feel "should have happened," absent some imagined amount of greed, and find the results unsatisfying.

It now should be clearer to us that "greed" is often nothing more than competition for resources playing out in markets with varied buyers.

In fact, there is no objective standard by which to determine when normal price competition goes too far and becomes greed. When challenged to set standards, people usually fall back on another hypothetical and imaginary concept: "fairness." As in, "it's not fair to charge so much."

Because fairness is situational and relative, everyone draws the line differently about what they think is fair. You can easily imagine how chaotic the world would become if transactions were governed by people's imaginary concepts of greed or fairness.

Back at our garage sale, the bidder who offered US$100 for your bike will certainly think it's unfair that someone is willing to pay US$200 for your bike. But is it unfair for you, as the seller, to accept the higher offer? Why exactly?

Fairness is in the eye of the beholder

Or perhaps the people promoting "fairness" object to something else entirely: that people have different levels of desire for the same goods. Assume both bidders have the same amount of money, but one likes biking more. Is it "fair" that the avid cyclist is willing to pay more for the bike?

Now, consider what would happen if we tried to promote "fairness" by eliminating "greed." As the seller at your garage sale, you could not consider potential buyers' greater desire to own your bike, or their greater ability to pay.

In fact, to be "fair" you'd have to know which person could afford the least or wanted the bike less, leading to absurd results.

- After hearing the bids for US$100 and US$200, the kid next door says "I've saved up US$50, but I also want to go to the movies, so I can't pay more than US$25. I still would like to have your bike."

- Is it fair to *anyone* if you sell your bike to the kid for US$25?

When we apply standards like "Don't be greedy," and "Be fair," it's a short step to conclude that people who have no disposable income are entitled to goods and services for free. Most people recognize that individuals and companies cannot simply give things away or they'd quickly go bankrupt.

People then arrive at the idea that companies should be allowed to earn a "reasonable" profit, but not "excess" profits. Does this sound to you like another way of saying "Don't earn more than an arbitrary amount I decide is fair?" Because that's exactly what it is.

Fairness, like beauty, is in the eye of the beholder. Fairness is relative and situational, which means that what we think is fair changes over time and changes depending on who is doing the comparing. What you think is fair is likely quite different than someone in different circumstances than you thinks is fair.

A much easier solution

If all this seems messy and complicated, don't worry. There is a fantastically simple and effective solution: Don't worry about greed or fairness but let market forces determine the prices of goods and services. Individuals expressing their individual preferences in pursuit of their own values effortlessly figure out what they're willing to pay.

In every other aspect of life, we give individuals freedom to decide how best to apply their interests and abilities. Some people are naturally talented, while some must work extra hard to achieve the same result. Others squander their gifts and waste their time.

If we value individual freedom, we must accept the necessary diversity of outcomes that comes with it.

Be well.

Chapter Twenty-Two

How Much Should Bosses Care About Employees?

Do I need to know what's going on in your life outside work for you to do your best work?

S ometimes you learn important things about yourself accidentally. I learned something about my management style relatively late in my career. We had announced my successor and one of my direct reports commented on the change.

He said, in all innocence, "The difference between your successor and you is that she cares about employees."

Upon first hearing this, I had to laugh out loud. It was so outrageous, but he said it so straightforwardly. Then I remembered my Stoic lesson about how to benefit from feedback: First, consider the source and, second, consider the truth of the statement.

In this case, the source was someone I trusted, which gave me pause. On reflection, I had to concede my friend was probably right.

That makes me sound like a terrible boss, and I suppose I was if my team was looking to me to be their friend providing emotional support. But the legal team was a well-functioning and high-performing team, highly regarded by the business.

This leaves me with the honest question of whether caring for your team is necessary for their, or your, success.

Some jobs don't teach leadership well

To understand many lawyers' leadership styles, it helps to reflect on our route to leading teams.

Lawyers who spend time in private practice early in their careers usually work independently. Yes, with a supervising partner and one or more senior associates. But junior associates are there to do grunt work and learn by doing. The senior lawyers are incredibly busy with little time and inclination for handholding.

I offer this as a description, not an excuse, for why lawyers typically learn little about team leadership in a law firm. Good role models are thin on the ground.

The lawyers who advance do so largely on the strength of their individual contributions. (And don't feel bad for lonely associates. Partners may feel even less inclined to help partners on matters with which they're not directly involved.)

Now let's say you've gone in-house. You may have started in-house directly out of law school, although I expect many in-house lawyers will have spent some time in private practice. If you did start in-house directly from law school, then everything you've learned about leadership you learned in the company environment.

The good news here is that you've got many more role models for good leaders across the business.

The lawyers leading legal teams have a certain seniority. This comes typically from a mix of private practice and in-house time. The more a legal leader's experience comes from private practice, the less likely they are to have developed strong team leadership skills.

If you've practiced for 10 or 20 years in a law firm, you are probably a great lawyer with impressive legal experience. But you have a steep learning curve in managing your new in-house colleagues.

I became a boss before I learned team leadership

I only spent five years in private practice before getting hired as the general counsel of a freshly-listed public company. I didn't come with too many bad habits, but I also brought no team leadership skills whatsoever.

Our legal team was small in those days. From the start, I treated my colleagues like trusted professionals. I left them alone to do their jobs, because that's how I performed best and because they knew more about their jobs than I did. I kept interactions minimal because I assumed that would help them work efficiently.

We tackled challenges and grew the team as the business grew. I invested what always seemed like disproportionate time in personnel matters: Budgets, salary rounds, target setting, progress checks, and annual evaluations. To say nothing of hiring new employees, having career development discussions, and finding ways to keep smart, ambitious lawyers suitably challenged but not overwhelmed.

I liked my colleagues immensely and was proud of how much they could do. I made it my personal mission to provide the best working environment I could, which to me meant focusing on strategically relevant topics that were valuable to the company. Our lean team members became awesomely qualified corporate generalists.

Because I was a young general counsel and stable in the role, we couldn't satisfy the ultimate ambition of some. Most who left went on to lead legal teams of their own. I think it says something about our environment that we created so many successful general counsels. It certainly wasn't because I was an empathic leader.

Sure, I got much better at human resource topics. I recognized time spent on employee topics as a wise investment. I am still in touch with almost everyone who spent time in our legal team. For me, this was always in aid of serving company interests.

I reminded myself often that the decisions we made were business decisions, not personal ones.

I could and did counsel underperforming employees, and fired many over my career, though thankfully very few in the legal team itself. I never liked it.

Looking back, my discomfort at disciplining or terminating colleagues probably contributed a lot to my being friendly with everyone but not friends. Otherwise, how could it not be personal?

Is caring for your employees necessary?

So now back to today's question. Is caring for your team necessary for their, or your, success? My answer is yes, but only to a point.

You must care a lot to be successful. The best leaders I know care deeply about their companies and their companies' fate, so they care about the individuals who work alongside them.

Can I care about your performance and want you to be successful without caring about your personal life?

Put differently, because that sounds callous, do I need to know what's going on in your life outside work for you to do your best work? I don't think so, but I could easily be convinced that more empathy would help an already great team perform better.

If a leader has the emotional bandwidth to delve into their team's private lives, wouldn't that be helpful? Helpful in the sense that people feel an even deeper connection to their colleagues? Feel understood and appreciated for more than their work product?

If it came naturally to me, I would have shown more interest. It doesn't, so I didn't.

I am thankful to my team that everything worked so well for so long. But I am also happy for my team that they now have a boss that cares for them as well.

Be well.

Chapter Twenty-Three

This Is Most Senior Leaders' Single Biggest Weakness

If you are serving in a C-suite role (or aspire to one), today's advice is something you probably haven't considered

I wish I had figured this one out while I was still serving as General Counsel of my S&P 500 company.

Looking back, it seems so obvious to me. But it wasn't at the time. And that's why I can say with confidence this is a weakness many senior leaders share.

I hope by raising this issue and discussing it openly, I encourage currently serving leaders to help themselves become even stronger in their roles.

So now you're wondering, "What's the big issue, James?" It's this:

Senior leaders have no obvious mentors within their companies

Senior leaders such as C-suite executives are in lonely roles. There is no one inside the company who understands all the issues that they face. And worse, they have little incentive to seek help from within.

I'll use my experience as General Counsel to illustrate.

The General Counsel cannot discuss many senior management and board-related topics with other legal team members, even senior ones. Confidentiality forbids. And until a person has held the responsibility themselves, they simply don't feel the weight of it the same way.

Other senior executives can no doubt relate. The chief financial officer or head of human resources have similar responsibilities they bear alone. But just as we won't understand the scope of the CFO's role and the intricacies of their concerns, so they do not understand ours.

Our boss is probably in the best position to understand our challenges. But do we really want to air uncertainties, stress, and frustration to our boss? We do not. So, we keep those thoughts to ourselves.

Interestingly, although the reverse is not the case, our boss can get sympathy from us. Every CEO who has felt the urge to vent their frustration at the latest board outrage will find the General Counsel to be most understanding.

Generic sympathy is nice, but not substantively helpful

We can and do have ways to find a sympathetic ear.

General Counsel probably have friends, maybe even people who mentored us along the way, with whom we feel comfortable airing our frustrations. And periodically letting off steam can be helpful.

Such people can give us generic advice about generic situations. They can also give us advice about managing our emotions and our expectations. We should be grateful for every assistance we get.

But the relief is temporary and anyway is a far cry from providing substantive aid. As in, "I'm facing a really tough decision. Let me tell you what I think and why I'm leaning this way. What are your impressions? What would you do if you were in my shoes?"

The solution is to talk to someone who knows exactly what you're feeling

Now some of you may be thinking, "That's why I go to industry meetings. The C-Suite club puts me next to other senior leaders for precisely this reason."

I used to think that as well. While those industry groups can be great, the interactions are fleeting and infrequent and everyone you meet is just as frantically busy as you are. In a day or two, they go back to their job, you go back to yours, and that was that.

No, what you want is someone who has not only walked a mile in your shoes but has time to focus on your issues. And you want them when you need them, and as much as you need them.

Yes, I'm referring to an executive coach. But not just any coach. You want as a coach a senior leader who knows from first-hand experience exactly what it feels like to make the decisions you're making. So a former CFO coach for CFOs, a former Head of HR for HR heads, and a former General Counsel for GCs.

Talking with someone who can provide substantive advice as well as emotional support is immensely powerful. Now instead of having to make critical decisions completely alone, you have a sounding board to help you work through the process.

It's obviously so helpful. Why don't more senior leaders use executive coaches? Why didn't I do it?

I can think of three reasons:

1. It never occurs to us to seek out such a coach;

2. We don't know they exist or where to find them; and

3. We're embarrassed to ask for help.

For smart people, senior leaders can be remarkably stubborn

Let's face it. No one makes it to the seniormost levels of leadership without healthy doses of independence, masochism, and competence.

You get used to doing things yourself (independence). Sometimes that means great effort and sacrifice because the situation demands it (masochism). And you wouldn't keep advancing if you weren't very good at it (competence).

Unfortunately, all three factors mean it rarely occurs to a senior leader that seeking tailored help is even an option.

Executive coaches who specialize in C-suite roles are rare

Executive coaches are plentiful. Chances are, as a senior leader you've recommended coaching more than once in connection with someone's development.

But coaches who focus on helping C-suite executives are rare. And those who were themselves C-suite executives even more so.

To conclude, there's a final reason senior leaders might not seek out coaching even upon acknowledging it could be hugely beneficial to them.

Senior leaders don't like to show weakness

Remember the independent, competent, but masochistic executive? There we go again. This reflects itself in our sometimes refusing to take simple steps to improve our lives.

I believe we can break out of this mindset. Ask yourself what you'd recommend to a colleague who wants to develop. Would you look down on them for taking advantage of the best resources on offer?

Of course not. If anything, you'd consider a person foolish for letting their pride or indifference hold back their career.

Don't handicap your chance of being the best executive you can be.

Be well.

Chapter Twenty-Four

Immortality Is a Foolish Wish

A few reflections on why living forever should be no one's desire

What drives the quest for immortality? An admixture of fear and greed. Fear of death. And greed for what seems sweet, for sensation without end. Both are foolish.

There's certainly no need to fear dying. Dying is easy. There's never been a person who failed the test. Willingly or not, they each made way for all of us who followed.

A person's greed for endless life is similarly short-sighted. With enough time, an immortal would suffer crushing boredom, having seen and done everything. Even thoughts and ideas would yield under the weight of time.

Worse, far worse, than an individual eternal's ennui would be the consequence of immortality on humankind. The end of death would mean the end of birth. If we add but a single soul per millennium, our numbers would approach infinity over an eternity.

How incredibly selfish (and arrogant) to think that humanity has reached its peak in us, such that we should not only live forever but be among the last who are born.

Value is found in scarcity. What we can obtain easily without limit, we do not value highly in possessing.

None of us knows our allotment of time, and that's what makes it precious. We strive, we love, and we live in equal measure to our appreciation that our time is scarce.

> *The world is fleeting; all things pass away; or is it we that pass and they that stay?* — Lucian

An ordered mind knows the value of life is precisely that it is limited.

What of those who accept they must pass away, but who wish to leave an indelible mark upon the world? Surely there number some such among authors. "My words will live on after me."

This is an interesting thought. How does it benefit us if some part of us remains after we are gone? Is it fame that goads us, even if it's posthumous? Is it a desire to influence the world, to make it better for all who come?

I suspect it's an ill-defined mix of emotions. We ameliorate the fear of dying by imagining some part of us or our influence will carry on. That, and the desire to make a mark is powerful and does not require that we remain to observe our handiwork.

It comforts me to remember that *everything* exists in a state of impermanent flux.

People will continue to come and go, as they always have. And that's the way it should be.

> *To what shall I compare this world? To the white wake behind a ship that has rowed away at dawn?* — Priest Mansei

Be well.

Chapter Twenty-Five

Five Ways to Ensure You'll Never Be Forgotten

Immortality is easier to achieve than ever

T oday I'll tell you how to set up your life such that it continues to be great long after your death.

The Athenian statesman Solon once said, "Count no man happy until he is dead." Until the whole of a person's life has played out, we don't know what misfortune may befall them.

For example, a person may be a famous, well-paid writer, but then suffer a bout of terrible herpes simplex that causes their entire body to break out in a rash, their spouse to divorce them, and all their friends to shun them. (And no, we are not subconsciously wishing that on anyone.)

Never mind herpes simplex, Aristotle took the concept even further. In discussing what made up the best-lived life, one of flourishing or happiness (in Greek, *eudaimonia*), we again judge the entirety of a person's life. But we also include the fate and fortune of their family and those close to them.

For example, a person may make their way to the highest political office of the most powerful country on Earth. But, completely hypothetically, if one son dies from brain cancer and another son is a drug-addled, bribe-taking, prostitute-frequenting, gun-form-application lying, non-tax-paying, (alleged) artist can we say the father is enjoying the most excellent and virtuous life?

No, it's far too risky to leave your eternal reputation in the hands of your potentially criminal relatives. To say nothing of the ones that are just waiting for you to pop off so they can spend your hard-earned money.

If you want to be judged a happy success, you should consider adopting one or more of these approachable paths to immortality (best used together):

1. Schedule stories to be published on your favorite platform for the rest of the century. On some, you can schedule a story to be published for decades from now.

2. To ensure you don't have to actually write all those stories, get ChatGPT to write them for you before it gets banned. (Haha! That'll never happen.) Better yet, pay for a customized AI that mimics your writing style so that no one ever need be deprived of your ongoing wit.

3. Leave your money in a trust that pays out to your relatives and their descendants only if, and to the extent, that they read and comment on your stories.

4. Direct your trust to send flowers to your descendants each year on the anniversary of your death with cards saying things like, "If only you'd been nicer to me, the money for this bouquet could have been yours" and "Maybe next year I'll just give you the money. In the meantime, better keep reading!"

5. Have your lawyers hire trolls in a third-world country (or ChatGPT, whichever is cheaper) to befriend your descendants on social media and tell stories about how they were great pals of yours, and how generous you were to them.

Well, this took a darker turn than I expected, but I can't see an easy way to pull it back, so I'm just going to end it there.

Be well.

Chapter Twenty-Six

We're All Big Babies

The world exists to satisfy our needs and wants, and because of this we will loudly express our displeasure if we are left wanting

I don't mean we are big babies in the sense of still wanting to eat ice cream for dinner, although this is both undeniable and understandable. I mean we are big babies in the sense that babies behave as if absolutely everything was about them.

If something happens that we do not like, we assume there was an intention to cause us harm. If I am offended, you must have intended to offend me.

Now, if this was our only similarity with babies, I would stop right here. But there is another similarity, namely that we think the world should immediately make all unpleasant things go away. I am hungry: Feed me! I am soiled: Change me! I am cold: Warm me! I am hot: Cool me! I am bored: Entertain me! You get the point.

How else to explain microaggressions and safe spaces? We have somehow managed to bring a generation of children into adulthood without ever leaving their babyness behind. And in the process, we have all embraced a bit of our inner baby as well.

I think it is time that we reminded ourselves of a few things. No one said age is a guarantee of maturity. Being an adult is hard, but we're the only ones who can do it. As the Buddha said:

No one saves us but ourselves. No one can and no one may. We ourselves must walk the path.

So the first step to maturing is recognizing that we have to do it ourselves.

But how do we leave the baby self behind? By taking responsibility for our thoughts, which will then help guide our actions. If you want to escape your safe space, and be freed of the pain of microaggressions, take heed of what Marcus Aurelius told himself:

Take away your opinion, and there is taken away the complaint 'I have been harmed.' Take away the complaint 'I have been harmed,' and the harm is taken away.

Though he was Emperor of the Roman Empire, Marcus Aurelius himself needed reinforcement, and I know we do as well. So I offer you this additional reminder on his behalf:

Cast away opinion: you are saved. Who then hinders you from casting it away?

Who indeed is stopping us from being the adults we want to be?

Best of all, I have it on good authority that even as an adult you can still have ice cream for dinner every now and then.

Be well.

Chapter Twenty-Seven

Skepticism is Safer Than Blind Trust

Your life improves when you understand the pervasive effect of incentives on human behavior. Skeptics can still be happy

Three advanced degrees, thirty years of work experience, and daily confirmations splashed across the headlines. All pointing to the vital role incentives play in our affairs. Still, I yearned for optimism and to trust my fellow humans.

Regular readers know I decry the folly of living in the land of wishful thinking. Of mistaking what we want to be true for what we experience. It's folly because continuing to trust in the face of regular disappointment doesn't make us kind. It makes us easy targets.

We stop being victims when we start being vigilant.

We can lessen the power of incentives over us, not by pretending they don't exist, but by accurately perceiving them.

Incentives drive human behavior, predictably and consistently

Humans are motivated to seek what they want (or at least think they want) and avoid what they do not. Understanding this explains most of what happens in life.

Don't let the simple formulation mislead you. This law holds great predictive power.

- People seek personal gain and place less weight on harm to others. Positive incentives predictably drive individual behavior.

- Fear of personal consequences prevents some behavior that harms others. Negative incentives only partially limit harmful behavior.

Concretely, people do things to make money and gain status or power (positive incentives). They avoid things they fear will get them in trouble — legally, financially, or reputationally (negative incentives).

What confuses us is that people sometimes appear to behave altruistically, they do things that demonstrate personal character, and they are not always villains.

This is a distraction. Incentives are always at play. When people behave well, it's not that they've become saints but that the incentives were aligned to encourage that behavior.

Nothing sets you up for victimhood more than mistaking examples of good behavior for evidence that most people are good.

When incentives are misaligned, bad things happen

The worst outcomes arise when large gains await those who face little risk of consequence for bad behavior.

Humans have significant control over the incentives at play. Individuals thus create opportunities for outsized gains at little risk. Think of every management team that first sets the business targets on which their bonus depends, then jiggers the business to meet those targets.

- Marketers push us to satisfy needs we didn't know we had

- Politicians incentivize us to fear their opponents

- Activists sensationalize science to influence narratives and gain power

- Content creators compete for our attention and falsehoods spread faster than truth

- Companies sell harmful products like alcohol, cigarettes, and junk food while glamorizing them to consumers

- Pharma companies propagandize doctors to peddle pharmaceuticals that turn us into lifelong consumers

- Criminals exploit loopholes in regulation and enforcement to steal our money

Everywhere we turn, incentives are at play. Someone's always playing an angle. If you don't spot the angle, you're the sucker being taken for a fool.

Does spotting the incentives turn one sour?

When you learn to spot misaligned incentives that drive selfish behavior, you see them everywhere. This can sour a person on their belief in humanity's fundamental goodness.

But it doesn't have to. Consider a spider, snake, or shark. Consider a hurricane, an earthquake, or a flood. All of these things exist in nature. They each wreak harm and havoc. So what? It's not personal, so why should you take them personally?

You don't need to consider a tornado to be aimed at just you to benefit from getting out of its way. You don't need to impute ill will to a hungry shark to see the wisdom in getting out of the water.

People respond to incentives. So what? Just because I won't let you hold my wallet doesn't mean I think you're a bad person. It just means I understand incentives.

I'm sold, James. How do I learn to spot incentives?

Here's a simple frame to identify relevant incentives about 80% of the time. Ask who gains and whether they could gain at your expense.

Another person's gains do not necessarily come at our expense. I may be perfectly happy spending my money to buy your product. (Although it is instructive to think carefully about why we want the product at all.)

Be alert for situations where someone benefits regardless of whether you benefit.

- When the financial advisor has sold you an annuity you may or may not need

- When the gym has signed you up for an annual subscription whether you set foot in the building

- When you pay an extra $10 a month to show your support for a community and get a gold star for your efforts

"Wait, wait!" I hear you cry. "I bought the annuity to get a guaranteed income stream." Sure. Was it the best product for you compared to other products? Did you realize your broker got a 9% fee for selling it to you?

"Well, I signed up to the gym to get healthy. How is that not in my benefit?" Come talk to me in a month.

"I show my support for the community here because I am the kind of person who selflessly supports others to make the world a better place."

Wonderful! I'd like to invite you to read more of my work. It's guaranteed to make the world better.

Be well

Chapter Twenty-Eight

What I Learned Negotiating for a Living

More important than winning, I learned when not to win

My team and I negotiated every kind of contract you can imagine. More than 10 million of them over the twenty-year period I served as General Counsel of an S&P 500 public company.

From tiny supply agreements to executive compensation deals. Sales agreements no one ever looked at again and acquisitions you've read about in the paper.

I learned how to get what I wanted most of the time. I was ruthless because I thought it was necessary. It took me years to gain the wisdom to approach negotiations mindfully.

I'd like to give you another way to think about getting what you want.

How I became a negotiation juggernaut

Although I possessed a fiercely determined streak from early on, I blossomed as a negotiator thanks to our Chairman and CEO.

He was one of those rare people who possessed a genuine reality distortion field in the sense that he often expected us to deliver impossible things. Just flat out, "No, that's not possible, not today and not in a million years."

What made him special or, now that I think about it, what made the team around him special is that we found a way to deliver on his impossible demands. Routinely, and far more often than we had any reason to expect.

Is it stressful going into a negotiation with a preposterous set of demands? Unbearably so. But the first time I achieved one of those herculean tasks, something happened to my view of the world and my self-confidence.

I learned I could do the impossible and that is an amazing feeling. Suddenly, merely difficult challenges seemed trivial in comparison.

What I learned from negotiation success

My negotiation success taught me several lessons that I've put to good use elsewhere in my life.

- My doubts are an unreliable guide to my capabilities

- I don't truly know what I can do until I commit to not failing

- It is thus appropriate to set my sights on Olympian heights

- It is also fair for me to ask others to deliver the seemingly impossible

It's not about what you ultimately achieve. It's about realizing that you should not place any limits on your or others' performance.

What a negotiation win won't teach you

Winning feels good, especially when it's against long odds. That winning feeling tells you nothing, however, about whether your goal was a worthy one.

We once pursued a competitor in an intellectual property infringement case. Mercilessly and relentlessly. We bent the world to our view and decisively won our case. Bankrupting our competitor, leading to their sale to another market participant, and creating the seeds for an even stronger future competitor.

Or consider one of the times we failed in a negotiation. This happened sometimes with monopolists (think software providers) or some of our largest customers.

They could, and often did, simply insist that we accept their terms. No discussion and certainly no negotiation.

Imagine how it feels being forced to submit to someone just because they have the power. Do you feel unfairly treated and taken advantage of? Check. Not only that but burning mad. And likely looking for a way to balance the scales again.

These are suboptimal outcomes for everyone, despite the initial appearance of winning. Focusing too much on a perceived win can blind us to the large set of outcomes that are better for one side without harming the other.

So what's a sounder way to approach negotiations?

Consider your negotiations (and your life) in context

My epiphany came when I realized that no negotiation is a one-off. There is always a before and an after.

If you are selling to a customer, do you expect to have an ongoing relationship with them? What will happen to that relationship if you press every advantage, just because you can?

Even the deals that seem entirely transactional, in the sense that the parties will never cross paths again, create ripples in how others perceive you. People will notice and interact with you accordingly.

And how you behave in negotiations comes to shape how you perceive yourself. Do you always win, no matter the cost? Or do you demonstrate kindness by being alert to opportunities to help others when it costs you but little?

These negotiation principles apply to our lives more broadly. We can pursue whatever we want in life. If we're willing to pay the cost, we can achieve just about anything we set our minds to.

My advice is to be careful viewing your goals as transactional or one-off. What you do to achieve your goals will affect what your life looks like once you've achieved them.

I still believe I can get whatever I want in a negotiation. But now I think more about what I should want before I go about getting it.

Be well.

Chapter Twenty-Nine

Bucket List, Eh. I'm Starting a F — It List

Letting go is so much more rewarding

What is a F — It List?

The F — It List contains not things I will never do, but things I commit to letting go.

1. **Jealousy**. About others' accomplishments, beauty, fame, etc. I celebrate success, knowing that another's success does not diminish mine or anyone else's.

2. **Dressing Well**. I'll have underpants and matching socks on. But no fashion statements will I make. And I'm OK with that.

3. **The Need to be Right**. It is so liberating to be able to think, and to say out loud, "But I could be wrong." I still have opinions, but I hold them less strongly.

4. **Looking Good Running Shirtless**. If ever this window of opportunity was open to me, I failed to notice it. Now when I notice runners who grabbed it, I smile and remind myself of item #1.

5. **The Need to Win**. I am competitive like crazy, and I credit it with carrying me far in my career. But I don't need to win every match. In fact, it's so much less stressful to acknowledge that coming in second (or third, or fourth) is totally fine.

6. **Feeling Guilty About My Sweet Tooth**. I know my enjoyment of chocolate (and cookies and ice cream) is just a collection of learned behaviors that I could unlearn. But I commit to the mighty task of letting go of the feeling I should.

7. **Everything Going According to Plan**. The unexpected is a gift, if we only look at it that way. When a plan goes awry, I now say, "Oh, what interesting opportunity has this change offered up?"

8. **Regret**. Our lives are the cumulated result of countless choices. I was active and thoughtful in all of them, certainly the big ones. Not everything went to plan (see item #7), but I will never make it worse by beating myself up.

9. **Worry About Things Outside My Control**. The Stoic key to happiness is understanding the distinction between what is within our control (or partly in our control) and what is outside our control. When you focus your thoughts on what you can control, great things happen.

10. **The TV Remote**. Just kidding, I'm never letting my spouse get ahold of that!

If you've ever daydreamed about your own bucket list, how about complementing it with a F — It List?

Be well.

Chapter Thirty

The Information Diet

The information we regularly consume is the biggest driver of our mental health

A lthough it's information that drives our mental health, we act as if what *happens* to us is formative.

If we devoted the same attention to our information diet as the food we eat, we could cultivate positive mental states. The three pillars to doing this are as follows:

1. Understanding why the information we consume is important to our well-being

2. Being aware of which types of consumption are harmful and which are beneficial

3. Creating an environment that allows for beneficial consumption

My thoughts on this are shaped by my psychology training, three decades practicing corporate law, and studying philosophy. More personally, by interacting with friends and colleagues around the world and seeing how their lives played out.

Here's what I've learned about people:

> Humans (short def.) – tell useful stories; also harmful ones.
> Most people do not distinguish sufficiently between the two.

From the same starting points and with similar abilities, some are happy and thriving while others are mired in difficulties. Why the difference? It comes down to their information diets.

1. Why the information we consume is important to our well-being

No one questions the importance of what we eat and how we exercise our bodies as fundamental drivers of physical health. Is it so hard to credit the information we feed our minds as influencing our mental health?

The stories we tell ourselves and each other define and amplify human incentives: What should we seek and why? What should we avoid and why?

Stories here mean all the ways we share information, from conversations to books to online content. Watching a video of a person mastering their guitar finger positions reinforces a positive incentive, just like seeing some fool singe off their eyebrows using gasoline to start their barbecue nicely demonstrates a negative incentive.

For much of human history, we shared information to improve the human condition. The great outpouring of human creativity forms the marketplace of ideas. Good ideas spread and become part of what we all know and understand.

Bad ideas also spread. We've put the name propaganda to it in the 20th century, but the concept of influencing how people think is older than that. For as long as people have lived and worked collaboratively, it has been beneficial to influence others' thinking because doing so influences their actions.

In other words, **information is never neutral**. This is so even if the messenger isn't trying to manipulate. Information changes minds, forms beliefs, and drives behavior.

You might have heard it expressed this way: As you think, so shall you become.

2. Harmful vs beneficial information types

Contrast drinking water sourced from a mountain spring with runoff from a chemical plant, the ooze leaking from a landfill, or a cup of tea laced with polonium. In the first case, pure and untainted. In the others, processed, polluted, and poisoned.

Think of the information you consume as similarly vital to your mental health and evaluate it in terms of purity and processing.

- **Purity** is a function of the source — is it new and untested or does it come from ancient wisdom, handed down for millennia?

- **Processing** is a function of how the information has been put to the service of an agenda. Does this come from a business that is selling you something or a politician who wants your votes and your money? Does it come from an entertainer who wants your attention?

You may have heard of the Standard American Diet, filled as it is with ultra-processed, addictive junk food. The same could be said of our information diet: Social media dominated, attention-driven, low on nutrition, highly processed, and addictive.

Our information diet should be free of such ultra-processed junk. Just as we're told to seek out natural, unprocessed, whole foods, we should seek out unadulterated sources of information.

Information that humans have been consuming and returning to for hundreds or thousands of years is much more likely to be healthy for us. This store of human wisdom has been digested, interpreted, and found nourishing and fit for human consumption.

This is not to say new information is necessarily harmful. We add valuable information to our stores every day. But to ferret out the worthy examples, we must sample mountains of dreck. Each week, month, and year that safely passes perform this filtering for us.

- We read Adam Smith with confidence today because his ideas have withstood the weight of time.

- We read Milton Friedman with admiration but some reservation because only a half-century has passed.

- We can readily identify those current economists as hacks whose words serve a partisan purpose.

3. Creating an environment that allows for beneficial consumption

Be careful of your exposure, particularly the media you choose.

We have no easy defense mechanisms to protect ourselves. Other than the passage of time, there is no food taster to tell us how much poison is in the dishes on offer. There is no test for foodborne viruses; our "fact-checkers" do a disservice to the name.

No government agency is coming to the rescue. The politicians and bureaucrats are among the worst propagandists seeking to control their unruly citizens. Social proof is no salve because trusted experts have fallen to partisan tribalism.

And we individuals are deeply untrustworthy. People will happily believe obvious falsehoods if they signal social status and demonstrate group membership and fidelity. What is a concerned person to do?

Here are affirmative steps to develop a healthy information diet:

- Consider going an Information Fast: Cut out ultra-processed information designed to lead us astray, including all legacy media and most social media.

- Commit to consuming more information from time-tested sources.

- You may consult guides who help you interpret that information, but only once they've proven themselves trustworthy to be part of your diet (i.e. not processed with an agenda).

Good luck in crafting your information diet.

Be well.

Chapter Thirty-One

Status Games You Can Win

Use the top 10% method to live a good life, make better decisions, and be happy

G ood things await those who make the right comparisons in life.

We can't turn off the comparison machine that's always running in our heads. The next best thing is choosing comparisons that make us feel great instead of feeding sad thoughts.

Why not play games you can win?

Feeling that we have status and a sense of self-worth is vital to our self-esteem, which drives many positive outcomes in life. The trick is to choose which status games we play rather than being inadvertently forced to play others' games.

Daily life offers so many options. Why not choose to play status games we can win? Let's consider "winning" as getting to the top 10% of a particular game (as we define it) because that level of performance will drive self-esteem.

It is simple to create games that suit this purpose. Examples:

- I have never been more than an average runner, in terms of speed, that is. So I focused on simply sticking with it. By running the Zurich marathon every year for 20 years in a row, I became one of just a handful of people who did so. Who cares how fast I am?

- Same thing with completing the World Marathon Majors and even getting a Guinness World Record in the process. That was similarly a function of simple determination and persistence. While others worried about finishing in under four hours or three hours, I just kept going.

If you can't compete on speed, compete on duration. If you can't win along one dimension, choose another that suits your abilities.

If this sounds delusional, as in, we're making up competitions that no one else even realizes or cares about, you're right. But if it makes us feel accomplished, it's a happy delusion that serves a purpose.

Your game hacks: Be Pragmatic, Stoic, and Machiavellian

As I'm using the terms here, the guidance is simple:

- Pragmatic means focusing on what works

- Stoic means looking within

- Machiavellian means being tactical

Be pragmatic ... or you can do stuff that doesn't work

Even assuming it's well-intentioned, most advice doesn't work. It's too generic (or too specific), too hard to implement, doesn't solve the underlying problem, only works temporarily, etc.

When I set up a global legal team for a new public company, I had to sift through mountains of advice. I found myself forced to adopt pragmatism as a guiding philosophy. No matter what others said, the only metric I valued was this: Does it work?

Does it work for me and my company? In our context, at this exact moment in time, with the specific challenges we're facing? If not, scrap it. If yes, figure out why and do more of it.

After some time, I began experimenting with pragmatism in my private life. What made one person succeed while other similarly situated people failed? Can others do it as well?

This may sound harsh but most people are not good role models, except as object lessons in what not to do. They waft through life like insects borne on the wind, flitting from one colorful flower to the next. Worse, many people act in demonstrably harmful ways, sabotaging themselves.

Whatever is important to you (health, wealth, career success, relationships, etc.), start by finding people who are good at it. Make them your focus. Spend time with them.

To give a personal example, I wanted to get fit after realizing in my early 30s I was overweight and unfit. I started hanging out with accomplished runners, which transformed my life.

Be Stoic — first for tough times and later for making times of your choosing

We will face tough times in our lives. Knowing this means we need not live in fear or lament when the tough times come.

Stoicism initially helped me by encouraging me to embrace hard things. I relished pushing boundaries and discovering I could do more than I first thought.

The combination of pragmatism and Stoicism results in profound effectiveness. For many years, I championed effectiveness at work and in private life.

If the story ended there, it would be perhaps interesting but unimportant. What shifted the plot was, ironically, too much success. How many people upon achieving all they once sought, ask themselves: "Is that all? I thought it would feel better. What's missing?"

What was missing, for me and I suspect for many, was meaning, the why of it all. That question led to another round of pragmatism — asking who is happy and satisfied in life and why. What are the things that contribute to living a good life?

How wonderful that answering this question led me right back to Stoicism. This time beyond the superficial finding that we can endure tough times to the underlying vein of wisdom: What we see is a function of where we look.

Put differently, our experience in life is shaped by how we think about it. And we have ultimate control of our thoughts. This allows us to not only overcome any situation but to determine what environments we find ourselves in altogether.

The power to look at what we want

Just like we are surrounded with mounds of advice, most of it ill-suited to our needs, we are invited to make comparisons that don't make us happy. Rather, the comparisons pushed on us are designed to make us feel lacking.

Marketers have made an art (and a giant industry) of emphasizing what's missing in our lives. They tell us that if we want to be happy, we must buy their products, drink their beverages, and download their apps. The immediate impact of this dark art is to make us unhappy.

Online influencers emphasize what we're missing by highlighting what they're enjoying. Lifestyles of the rich and famous satisfy our voyeuristic instincts while driving dissatisfaction.

This comparison group is hopelessly large, often the whole country if not the entire world. What are the chances you are the luckiest, wealthiest, most attractive, and most accomplished person among millions or billions?

Would you rather play games you can win or games where you're almost certain to be the sucker? Put that way, few would knowingly choose games they're designed to lose. Yet accepting what marketers and social media offer sets us on the path to disillusionment.

Be Machiavellian by choosing battles you can win

Now we come to the beating heart of it, dear reader. If finding happiness is a meaningful pursuit, then directing our thoughts is a path to doing so.

The comparison machine constantly running in our heads is the greatest risk to happiness, always threatening to lead us astray by spotting how often we fall short.

We can put happiness in our hands by grabbing control of the comparison machine. Stoicism tells us we can choose how to direct our thoughts and Machiavellism points the way forward: We shall only play status games we can win.

Find areas where your current or achievable performance automatically puts you in the top 10%.

This approach works because it feeds the comparison engine. The engine is blind. It doesn't know whether some accomplishments are worth more than others. It only knows whether you're excelling in the areas it's been trained to look at.

Here are some ways to collect status by playing this game:

- **Education** — Did you do well in school or earn an advanced degree?

- **Work** — Are you working, does your company value you, do you have management responsibilities?

- **Finances** — How do your earnings and savings compare to the rest of the globe? You'd be surprised how little it takes to be in the global top 10%

- **Physical aspects** — Are you tall, do you have blond hair or blue eyes?

- **Fitness** — Do you have a healthy weight, are you mobile, have you made it to the age of 40?

- **Anything else** — Do you have a fine sense of humor, a huge collection of matchbooks, or come from a tiny country? Anything that makes you uniquely you can serve as your path to relative status.

It does not matter what you choose to focus on, just that you measure up relatively well. Unhappy people look too long at the areas where they fall short. Happy people appreciate what makes them stand out.

To live a good life and find happiness, learn to direct your attention to the ways you are lucky enough to already be winning. I've never met anyone who wasn't in the top 10% at something — what's your game?

Be well.

Chapter Thirty-Two

The Boss Toolkit: When My Best Employees Couldn't Prioritize

Was I a terrible boss? It sure looked that way, but I had a purpose behind my behavior

W hat do you do as a manager with a promising employee who isn't getting their work done? Although there are many causes, I found one reliable cure: Pile them high with more work.

It's counter-intuitive and risky because, in the near term, you're just adding to their stress and risking a blowup or burnout. But if you trust your instinct that your employee has potential and is up for it, challenging them is a pragmatic way to help them develop their prioritization skills.

Although it looks cruel, the employee and boss each benefit from the practice because it usually makes the employee into a great performer.

When perfectionists hurt themselves

I hired many junior lawyers over my career. I came to dread the first six months after they joined.

These were smart, hard-working, and high-performing professionals, used to excelling at whatever they tackled. Ironically, those attributes made them terrible in-house lawyers, at least initially.

Company lawyers perform best when they deliver what the business needs. While this may sound obvious to you, for lawyers it can be a real shift in mindset. Our training teaches us to be careful and precise. Words matter and details matter. So we obsess over every little thing.

The problem is that the business neither needs nor wants obsessive nitpicking on much of what its in-house lawyers do. Negotiations, contracts, and risk management — they all benefit from a careful approach, but not an obsessive one.

Or as you may have heard in other contexts, good is good enough.

In the case of the junior lawyers we hired to review commercial contracts, it was a disaster to see them spending a week reviewing and marking up a single agreement to make it near-perfect when they should have been capable of handling five or 10 contracts a day.

The solution is to make perfectionism impossible

The simplest way to do this is to pile on the work. Don't give them one contract at a time, give them five, ten, or even twenty. Then set aggressive deadlines that they must meet.

Let them work it out.

Initially, this will create immense pressure and stress. That's when their risk of burnout is greatest. They'll start by maintaining their old, impossible standard of perfection and working all the hours of the day.

Some will quickly figure out productivity shortcuts. This comes from experience, practice, and expediency.

- They realize much of the work is repetitive, so comments on one type of clause will work on all agreements with that clause.

- They experience better results negotiating some clauses than others, so learn which types of clauses are more easily dealt with.

- And they get a sense (from colleagues and you, the boss) of what types of clauses the business cares about and which ones are less important. That naturally guides their efforts.

Other employees need help in seeing the shortcuts. This is also when you can give guidance as the manager. After loading up an employee and letting them try to manage the workload, observe who struggles.

Sit down with your underwater employees and review an agreement with them. Show them how you would do it and why. If they are as intelligent and talented as you suspect, they will quickly grasp the principles.

Isn't there another way?

I've learned that the gentle explanation rarely works in the absence of pressure. For all those wondering why the boss doesn't explain to employees the process in advance, the boss does but the employee doesn't listen or the lesson doesn't stick.

The pressure of impossible deadlines (under the old, perfectionist system) makes the brightest students pay the closest attention.

It is not kindness to let employees flounder. It does employees no favors to hold them to lower standards. Good employees don't mind working, especially when they feel that what they're doing is both challenging and valuable.

So I say it's correct to put employees under pressure to teach them to prioritize. They'll thank you for it later.

Be well.

www.ingramcontent.com/pod-product-compliance
Lightning Source LLC
Chambersburg PA
CBHW060329050426
42449CB00011B/2710